EBURY PRESS
THE MILLENNIAL YOGI

Deepam Chatterjee is a retired Indian Army captain. He took up film-making after a debilitating spinal injury compelled him to leave the army. It was during this period that he spent time with various spiritual teachers, including the Dalai Lama. Later, he trained under Sri Sri Ravi Shankar and taught the Art of Living courses before embarking on a journey of self-exploration.

A keen researcher as well as chronicler of oral narratives, Deepam writes and lectures on Hindu thought, meditation, spirituality, mysticism, mythology and wellness. He has translated a significant body of Sanskrit works into accessible English for young readers and mainstream audiences. His work appears regularly in newspapers and periodicals across the country. You can connect with him on Instagram @deepam.chatterjee.

T0148903

ADVANCE PRAISE FOR THE BOOK

'Captain Deepam Chatterjee's *The Millennial Yogi* guides the reader through the cathartic transformation of a young entrepreneur after his chance meeting with a mystic monk, whose teachings lead the protagonist on a passionate quest for meaning in everyday life. A fascinating account of spiritual and emotional catharsis, all the more timely in today's turbulent times'—Shashi Tharoor, member of Parliament

'I am glad that Deepam has at last made his debut as a novelist. His first novel takes the reader through a fascinating dual spiritual journey. I congratulate him on this novel and wish him well in the future' —Karan Singh, author, statesman, educationist and environmentalist

'I have seen Deepam transform from a young officer into a teacher of mysticism and meditation. I listen to his discourses with great fascination as they are getting better by the day. Deepam's debut book, *The Millennial Yogi*, is an engrossing and thought-provoking read. I am sure many more such books will flow from his pen in years to come'—General N.C. Vij, former chief of the army staff

'Deepam's debut book, *The Millennial Yogi*, is an intriguing read, interspersed with the music and poetry from many mystical traditions of India, including Sufi and Baul couplets. This modern parable is extremely relatable, as it is based upon the theme of reclaiming our life when we are down. Deepam's writing is crisp, intriguing and engaging. The story traverses two different eras and teaching traditions, and in parts it reminds me of my own life and student days with my teachers. I am certain that *The Millennial Yogi* will be the first in a long series of books by Deepam Chatterjee'—Shankar Mahadevan, singer, composer and actor

'Deepam Chatterjee is the rare army officer who has taken the road less travelled. He has been teaching mysticism and meditation for many years. In *The Millennial Yogi*, he has poured a lifetime of his life experiences. Deepam has woven a beautiful parable about Jay, a young man whose intense ambition to attain success at any cost leads him to complete ruin. However, in a serendipitous moment, he meets his mentor Vini, who helps Jay find meaning and purpose. Life is beautiful and we must learn to make the best of what we have, rather than focusing on what we don't. Deepam's book compels us to ponder the deepest of questions—what is the purpose of our lives? We all struggle with adversities. How we deal with them makes or breaks us. Nothing is impossible. Through *The Millennial Yogi*, Deepam has underlined this message. Where there's will, there's a way. If we have the will, we can find our inner strength and conquer the whole world'—Deepa Malik, Padma Shri, Khel Ratna and Arjuna awardee, and co-founder, Wheeling Happiness Foundation

'I am very happy and excited about my friend Deepam's debut book, *The Millennial Yogi*. It's the kind of book that arrives rarely and leaves an everlasting imprint on the landscape of literary fiction. In the tradition of *The Monk Who Sold His Ferrari* and *The Alchemist*, Deepam has woven a very powerful message about clawing back from the brink, when one is completely down and out, and reclaiming one's life. For me, the ease with which Deepam writes the visually engrossing story demonstrates his grasp of story structure, and it has a huge potential to be adapted for the large screen. I am eager to read more interesting stories from Deepam Chatterjee. Keep 'em coming, my dear friend!'—Raj Nayak, founder, House of Cheer, media maven and happiness evangelist

'Moving and thought-provoking'—Stuti Changle, bestselling author of *You Only Live Once*

THE
MILLENNIAL
Yogi

A modern-day parable
about reclaiming one's life

DEEPAM CHATTERJEE

EBURY
PRESS

An imprint of Penguin Random House

EBURY PRESS

USA | Canada | UK | Ireland | Australia
New Zealand | India | South Africa | China

Ebury Press is part of the Penguin Random House group of companies
whose addresses can be found at global.penguinrandomhouse.com

Published by Penguin Random House India Pvt. Ltd
4th Floor, Capital Tower 1, MG Road,
Gurugram 122 002, Haryana, India

First published in Ebury Press by Penguin Random House India 2022

Copyright © Deepam Chatterjee 2022

ISBN 9780143456148

Typeset in Sabon by Manipal Technologies Limited, Manipal

www.penguin.co.in

To my parents, Manjushree and Varun

*You have inspired and encouraged me
to be happy, always*

Contents

Preface

'If I have seen further, it is by standing on the shoulders of giants.'

—Isaac Newton

What is written well is so because we have been taught by great teachers. They instilled in me a sense of wonder and the joy of reading. My childhood memories are filled with books. From the classics to mysteries and tales of adventure, I wanted to read everything. And I read really fast, retaining almost everything, which I thought was normal for everyone. From Enid Blyton to Isaac Asimov, Carl Sagan, Erich von Däniken and Arthur Conan Doyle, I had read them all before I turned twelve. The first book that I remember being gifted on my birthday—and this (gifting me books) became a norm until very recently, after over 3000 books that I cannot begin to part with—was *A Tale of Two Cities*.

When my mother took us to Arera Colony, Bhopal, to her parental home, I had a fascinating time exploring the large house. It had a huge terrace, with a small storeroom on one side. Half of the rest of the terrace was covered with a roof made of translucent green plastic sheets, and there was a room with an ancient Remington typewriter that intrigued me. My grandfather was a great botanist and wrote, or rather typed, his books and papers in there.

One day, when my panic-stricken family couldn't find me for hours, a search party went around the colony, frantically looking for me. Finally, my grandmother, a feisty lady, found me in the terrace storeroom, sitting on top of a cement shelf, high above the floor, a few feet below the roof, rummaging through old books in both Hindi and English. How I had climbed up, and not slipped and fallen down, I really do not know.

At my father's childhood home in New Alipore, Calcutta, there was a massive glass-paned book cupboard, with beautiful gold-embossed *Rachanabalis* of Bankim Chandra Chatterjee, Sarat Chandra Chattopadhyay, Rabindranath Thakur and many more, both in Bangla and English.

I had no scruples about purloining library books. If I liked a book, I just decided not to return it. How many times I was chased by librarians and comic book owners, I cannot remember. The first book fair that I went to at Pragati Maidan, New Delhi, was as a ten-year-old. My only memory of that fair is of stealing two Archie comics, and of being chased halfway to the exit by the shopkeeper's terribly angry assistant. We were some five or six of us, young and reckless, with a fanatical love for reading.

My mother and father have been ardent readers, and we've always had well-worn copies of the complete works of Shakespeare, Dickens, Jane Austen, the Brontës, Swift and Dumas at home, jostling with books by Arthur Hailey, Desmond Bagley, Alistair MacLean, Barbara Cartland and even Harold Robbins. It goes without saying that I read everything I could lay my hands on as I grew up. Half a dozen heavy dictionaries and thesauri stare back at me sadly, unopened for decades.

My tryst with Hindi poetry began parallelly, with my love for reading Mahadevi Verma and Jaishankar Prasad (whom I pay tribute to, as Jay, in this book), followed by Ramdhari Singh Dinkar, Subhadra Kumari Chauhan. Hindi literature has a completely different flavour, and I was left mesmerized by the colourful imagery that was percolated into the writings of Acharya Chatursen, Vrindavan Lal Varma, Dharamvir Bharati and Rangeya Raghav.

As I grew older, I veered towards introspective, philosophical and spiritual literature, and this became the main fodder for me after I began understanding the deeper nuances of Maugham, Fitzgerald and Hemingway on the one hand, and Premchand, Nirala, Amrita Pritam and Harivansh Rai Bachchan on the other. Their influence is evident in my writings.

I soon graduated to reading Urdu poetry in Devanagari, as I cannot read the original script, and to reading translated books. What a fascinating world we live in! I wanted to learn every new language so that I would be able to read the writings in the original, but alas, so little time, and so much to read!

Delving deeper beyond language, I began exploring spiritual and mystical poetry and was slowly led to learn, and then teach, the devotion-soaked writings of the Bhakti saints, the exclamations of amazement and joy of the Advaitins, and began to realize the infinite depth of the awakened ones. Sufi, Zen, Taoist and Vedanta writings eventually directed me towards the Upanishads and the Vedas. Seeking the ultimate, I had reached the beginning of words, *seen* by the rishis in deep meditation and stillness. The yearning to attain what they experienced has taken me beyond words . . .

And yet I write, to explore and express the inexpressible.

> *Seeking the beginning,*
> *At the source of the word,*
> *There is pure silence . . .*

> *And, the sincere seeker,*
> *Is at a loss for words . . .*

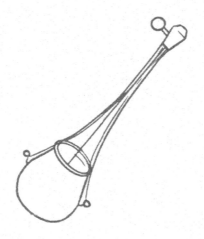

Prologue

The Taut String

'Look, Sagar, I can't help it. We'll need to reschedule ...
What . . .? Sagar, I don't care if he has Eric Clapton
coming there to teach him . . . Tell that idiot to shove
his guitar up you know where!'

Jayshankar Prasad, or Jay, scowled as he shouted
into his phone, his eyes searching for a place to sit
in the crowded multi-airline lounge. The young
and brilliant entrepreneur had been up till 2 a.m.
preparing for a vital meeting, slept for two hours and
then rushed for his flight to Mumbai at 6 a.m. in the
morning, only to be told that a technical snag had
led to a two-hour delay of his flight. And now this
Hooda, some distant cousin of the sports minister's
wife, was refusing to reschedule because of some
confounded guitar class!

Jay spotted a table for two that appeared to be
unoccupied. The tall and lanky twenty-eight-year-old
didn't notice the small suitcase tucked away beside a

chair on the far side as he rapidly walked towards the table and, still talking on the phone, pulled the other chair out. He threw his jacket on the back of the chair, plonked his overnighter on the floor and sat down, all in a single fluid motion.

'. . . I know, I know! He can do the meeting next week, and you will manage all the paperwork. But that doesn't help, Sagar! What if he changes his mind tomorrow? We are slogging our asses off. You know that. It's not my bloody fault that the flight is delayed, bro. My Mumbai meeting is also very important. I can't cancel it. I shall only be able to catch the twelve o'clock flight back now. Which means I'll be back in Delhi around one thirty at the earliest!'

As Jay continued talking agitatedly, a middle-aged man walked up to the table. In one hand, he was carrying a small plate which had a couple of sandwiches, some fruit and a paper cup. In his other hand, the man held a strange-looking wooden instrument that seemed vaguely familiar. Jay eyed him curiously while continuing to talk on the phone.

The man had a gentle smile playing on his lips, and the moment Jay stopped talking to hear Sagar out, he pointed to the empty chair and mouthed silently, 'May I sit here?'

Jay grudgingly assented, nodding wordlessly. The man was wearing a cotton dhoti and a cream bush shirt. He appeared to be glowing with serenity and peace. Jay noticed that under the plate, precariously balanced, the man was clutching what looked like his passport and wallet.

The man smiled as he reverentially placed the wooden instrument to his left, gingerly kept his plate down in the centre, placed his passport and wallet on his right, almost at the edge of the small table, gently pulled the chair out and sat down. He then picked the paper cup and placed it next to the instrument, before once again picking the plate up and offering the contents to Jay, who refused, distractedly shaking his free hand as he talked on the phone. As Jay watched him from the corner of his eye, the man slowly sipped water from the paper cup, took a small bite from one sandwich and then began to gently twist and untwist some kind of wooden knob on the odd-looking instrument, alternately tightening and loosening its single string. The man's slow, zen-like actions seemed strangely calming to Jay.

'. . . look Sagar, you'd better get the guy to meet me in the afternoon . . . Tell him, otherwise the deal's off . . . I will not give him a single rupee . . . I am ready to meet him as soon as I land. 3 p.m., 4 p.m., whenever. But I cannot meet him tomorrow morning. I have other engagements . . . TO HELL WITH HIS GUITAR CLASS AND HIS HIGH TEA!' Jay banged the phone down angrily, and ended up knocking the man's wallet and passport off the table. The man gave a start, and the string of the instrument snapped with a loud twang.

'Oh! I am so sorry!' Jay mouthed, in nearly the same high pitch that he had been shouting in a moment ago. He realized that it was his angry outburst that had caused the chaos. He quickly bent down to pick up the man's passport, which seemed quite thick. It lay open on the floor, face-down, and a sheet of paper had slipped out of it. Jay picked these up, and his eyes caught the man's name as he put the piece of paper back inside and closed the passport. Ashwini Kumar Singh. The man, too, bent over and picked his wallet up.

They both straightened up, and Jay handed the passport back to the man, who was still smiling gently. Jay once again said, 'I am really sorry.'

'Don't worry at all,' the man replied. 'Often, when we get angry, we lose awareness of things around us.' He went back to his instrument and gradually began to unwind the broken string from one end.

The man was completely engrossed in his work. Jay hesitated a bit before he said, 'I will pay you for the string.'

'Don't worry, I have a spare. The string needed changing anyway.'

Jay watched the man curiously as he removed the string.

'You know why the string snapped?' the man asked, without looking up.

Jay replied with a question. 'Because it was old and rusty?'

The man said, 'Old, yes. It has been a while since I changed it. But it wasn't rusty. I have been playing it continuously for days without giving it any rest.' The man spoke of the instrument as if it were a living thing, Jay thought.

'Maybe the string had become too tired and decided that it was time to go.' The man laughed. 'But more importantly,' he continued in a serious tone as he worked on the instrument, 'the string snapped because it was taut, and suddenly, I tightened it further, instead of loosening it.'

'Yes, all my fault,' Jay said.

'Yes and no,' the man said with a smile, looking up. 'I too should have been more careful.'

Oddly, Jay felt a bit calmer as he talked with this strangely unperturbed man. There was something familiar about the lined face. Jay felt that he had met the man before but couldn't seem to place him.

'Just like this string, we all need tending. When we are tense, we need to find ways to loosen up. Or we just might snap one day.'

The man reminded Jay of a basic fact of life. He knew that he needed to slow down, but his life was moving at a breakneck pace. Suddenly, he remembered a recurring dream of his . . .

It's pretty dark, probably late evening, and he's running on a long platform, alongside a moving train, desperately trying to jump inside. He has two big and heavy suitcases that he is gripping tightly in both hands.

Almost immediately, he is accosted by a large number of filthy beggars who begin wailing and clawing at him, tearing at his clothes, not letting him run any faster. He keeps trying to push them away, but many more loathsome and horrible-looking beggars appear and pull at him, not letting him get on the train.

He runs harder, nearly escaping the clamouring crowd of beggars as the train rushes away, going faster and faster.

His anxiety grows. He knows that he has to catch that train. It's going to take him somewhere very important. He doesn't know where, but he must get to that place. He has to get away from this terrible hellhole, leaving all these people behind.

Suddenly, the platform ends, and he skids to a stop right at the edge, nearly falling to his death as he helplessly watches the train speed away, now far beyond his reach . . .

He'd had this dream a hundred times, and he always woke up sweating, with his heart thumping. He knew that he would never catch that train.

'There! That's done.' The man smiled at Jay, who was still staring at him, although his mind had been elsewhere. Jay jerked back to the present as the man asked, 'Is there something wrong?'

Jay realized he'd been staring, shook his head and opened his mouth to say something but decided not to. The man smiled once more as he sipped water. 'Please don't hesitate,' he said. 'Tell me what you wanted to say.'

'Sir, I saw your name on the passport. And your face is very familiar too. Are you Ash? The *famous* Ashwini Kumar Singh?'

The man shook his head and smiled softly. 'Famous? I really have no idea. I used to be called by that name long ago. Seems like another lifetime . . .' He then went on to recite,

'Bekhudi le gayee kahaan humko,
Der se intezaar hai apnaa.

Kuchh nahin hum misaal-e-anqaa lek,
Shahar-shahar ishtihaar hai apnaa!'

Jay looked confused. The man chuckled softly and said,

'Where has this rapturous ecstasy taken me,
I have waited very long to meet myself.
Nothing am I, but an instance of the unattainable,
and yet,
I am being talked about in towns and cities!'

'People call me Vini nowadays,' he continued, smiling. 'But I really don't know who I am . . .' He looked directly into Jay's eyes. 'My guru gave me this name, which means "weaved" in Pali, the language the Buddha spoke.'

Jay looked at Vini quizzically. He felt a bit disconcerted looking directly into Vini's eyes. There was a strange magnetic pull in them. He realized that the man in front of him was none other than the famous business mogul Ash, who had disappeared years ago. But this man seemed to be a completely different person.

'You disappeared over twenty years ago. Everybody believes you're dead!'

'And they are so right! Ash died long ago.' Vini smiled.

'Where did you go, sir? What happened? I must tell you that I was a fan of yours. You disappeared when I was a kid! I have read everything about you. You were . . . are a maverick! You had such a unique style of working. In fact, during my IIM days, I often quoted you in my presentations. You were India's answer to Jack Welch,' Jay spoke excitedly. 'I had even written an article on you for our college magazine. I'd made a scrapbook of newspaper cuttings and magazine articles on you! I kept track of your stupendous rise to power, your sudden fall and subsequent disappearance. We all believed that you had been killed by rivals as the body was never found! Obviously! You have been alive all this while. And now, around . . . twenty-three years later, I am sitting in front of you! Wow! This is unbelievable!'

Vini nodded silently as he leaned down to pull out his suitcase. Jay noticed it for the first time. 'You were sitting here before I came and grabbed the table! I am really sorry, sir. I should have checked. By the way, my name is Jay. Jayshankar Prasad Sharma.'

Vini looked up and said softly, 'That's okay, Jay. This is a public place.'

Jay asked Vini, 'Where had you gone sir? Twenty-three years is a long, long time.'

Vini was reticent. 'Well, I travelled, and I learnt a lot of new things. But nothing that would make me money!' Vini smiled gently, his eyes twinkling. He continued, 'My story is not very interesting, Jay. No exciting adventures like Sinbad or Columbus. You seem to have a very interesting life. Tell me a bit about your work.'

Jay animatedly began to share how he had set up ALSOL, his turnkey solutions company, and that he had a number of projects in the pipeline. He said that although there was a lot of pressure on him all the time, he enjoyed his work since he was making good money.

Vini nodded as he unzipped the side flap of his suitcase, reached into it and, after rummaging a bit, took out a leather pouch. He placed the pouch on the table, opened it and pulled out a paper sachet that he tore open. There was a coiled metal wire inside.

'May I know what this instrument is? I have seen pictures of it but cannot recall what it's called.'

Vini smiled and deftly began to attach the string to the instrument. He spoke softly, 'This instrument is called the ektara. It was given to me by my gurudev. It represents the soul.' He paused and looked up. 'We are all wandering in search of happiness, aren't we?'

Jay nodded.

Vini continued fitting the string on the ektara. He plucked at the string while loosening and tightening it alternately, using a wooden knob, which protruded from the narrow end of the instrument. 'Whatever we do is to find happiness and joy. I went off on my own journey seeking joy. Even you, Jay, are on a journey seeking happiness. Don't you think?'

Jay said, 'Right now, I don't really feel anywhere close to being happy. Too much tension. This two-hour delay has completely ruined my schedule.'

'And yet, you are sitting here, at six thirty in the morning, waiting to get somewhere as quickly as possible. Aren't you doing all this to gain happiness?' Vini chuckled as he plucked at the string, readjusting its tautness.

'I don't understand, sir.'

'Call me Vini, please. What I mean is, all this running, all day long, day after day, week after week, month after month, is so that you achieve something, isn't it?'

'Absolutely. If my project goes through, I will make good money for my company, and a big name for myself!'

'Ah! And that will make you happy, will it not?'

Jay nodded.

'You are in this present situation which is pretty uncomfortable, so that you will become happy some day in the future, isn't it?'

Jay nodded again, unsure where the conversation was going.

'Why not be happy right now? Why do you wait for something to happen, and decide that only then you'll be happy? Why do you postpone happiness?'

Jay stared at Vini with his mouth slightly open, as if he'd been punched in the face.

'Do you sleep well?' Vini continued.

'Excuse me?'

'Do you get good sleep?'

Hardly, sir . . . Vini. Too many things to think about!' Jay grinned sheepishly and fiddled with his phone.

Vini nodded. 'You seem quite excited about your work. That's a good thing. Do you meditate?'

'Haha! I tried to, a couple of times. Can't seem to sit still. But I love going for a run and hitting the gym whenever I get the time. And I love listening to Coldplay. Soothes my nerves.'

Vini nodded. He loosened the ektara string a bit more and said, 'You know, Jay, this ektara string is like us all. You make it too tight and it snaps, or the ektara itself might crack; and, if the string is too loose, you'd be unable to play any tune on the ektara. The same is the case with our mind and body. Too much tension will damage us, and too little stress will make us lazy and useless.'

Without looking up, Vini continued, 'Just like this string, we all need a little adjustment, time and again. A little tightening, a little loosening. Just like you do right now. Otherwise, you will snap—like that old string. Stress is important, if kept in control and balance. Something already in tension will be totally devastated if put under further pressure . . . Ah! That is perfect.' Vini plucked at the ektara and hummed a tune softly.

'Bulleya! Ki jaana main kaun!

Na main momin vich maseetaan,
Na main vich kufar diyan reetaan,
Na main paakaan vich paleetaan,
Na main Moosa na Firown!

Bulleya! Ki jaana main kaun!'

Jay watched Vini with astonishment. He whispered in awe, 'What did you sing? It sounded so beautiful. Really.'

Vini said, 'This is a beautiful Sufi poem of Baba Bulleh Shah. He was a wandering saint, who sang songs of awakening. In this poem, Bulleh Shah is talking to himself. Bulleya, as he usually addressed himself, contemplates who he really is, after having realized the self.'

Vini translated what he had sung for the mesmerized Jay.

'O Bulleya! Who knows, who I am!

Not a believer praying in the mosque am I,
Nor a non-believer who follows false rituals,
Nor the unsullied one in the midst of the impure,
Neither Moses, nor the Pharaoh!

O Bulleya! Who knows, who I am!'

'That was totally awesome, Vini! When did you learn to sing so beautifully?'

'I have never learnt music, Jay. With the blessings of my master, I share my joy through the words of free spirits. My soul dances in tune with their words, and music flows . . .'

Jay pressed him for more details. 'Please tell me more about yourself. Who is your master? What did you learn from him? How are you so joyful and happy?'

Vini smiled. 'This isn't the best place or the right time to talk about such things, Jay. We will surely meet once I get back to India. In fact, I am keen to meet and chat with you again. In the meanwhile, can I request that you keep my earlier identity to yourself? I do not identify with it any more and really do not wish to be in the limelight.'

'Yes, Vini, I will certainly respect your wish,' Jay said.

'I am on my way to a seminar on mystic music in Prague and need to get some things organized, once I've had some breakfast.'

'Oh! I am so sorry, Vini! I didn't realize that you too must be waiting to board a flight! Please carry on!'

'One important thing I have learnt in these years, Jay, is that if you let things be, they let you be. If you don't interfere with the workings of the divine plan, things generally work out for the best.'

Jay became pensive as Vini resumed eating. For a few moments, he watched Vini eat his food unhurriedly and in complete silence, processing all that had occurred in the last ten minutes. Then, Jay's phone beeped, and he started reading his messages.

All of a sudden, an agitated attendant rushed into the lounge, announcing Jay's name. The technical snag had been repaired an hour early and his flight was about to depart. They had been looking for him everywhere. This being a silent airport, no announcements were made, and passengers needed to keep a lookout themselves. The attendant admonished Jay as he hurriedly got up to leave.

Jay's phone beeped again, and he laughed seeing the message. His meeting with the industrialist would now happen at the Mumbai airport itself. The guy had to leave for Chennai all of a sudden, and wanted Jay to wait at the departure lounge for him. This meant that Jay could take his scheduled flight back to Delhi and meet the minister's wife's cousin at the earlier designated time. By now, Jay had forgotten Vini.

Lost in his thoughts, he quickly picked up his jacket and overnighter, and turned to follow the impatient attendant while calling Sagar on the phone. Vini smiled to himself as he overheard Jay's cheerful tone.

'Hey, Sagar . . . You haven't spoken to Hooda yet? Great! No, no! Don't apologize, buddy! And don't say anything to him when he wakes up. I am sorted. Will meet him at 12.30 p.m. as planned . . . How did I manage it? Hahaha! *I just let things be*. And everything simply fell into place! Ciao, Sagar. Love ya!'

Jay had a spring in his step as he strode behind the attendant at a brisk pace, eager to catch his flight. He only remembered his chance meeting with Vini when he was settling into his business-class window seat. Jay realized that in the hurry to get to his flight, he had neither taken Vini's phone number, nor his address.

1

A Nasty Man

Vini returned to India in a week. Day was just breaking when his taxi came to a halt on the dirt road, which snaked into the rundown locality that had been his home for the last couple of years. Quite a few children were already up and about, skipping as they went towards the bus stop behind the swanky mall that had come up on land that had once belonged to their forefathers.

Vini got out of the vehicle. He had his trolley in one hand and his ektara in the other, packed in a bag. He thanked the taxi driver, who waved as the car began its bumpy ride back to the main road, a few hundred metres away. Vini watched the children as they raced behind the car, chattering and giggling. A couple of startled dogs began barking and joined the race; they had grown up with the kids. 'How carefree those days of innocence were!' Vini thought to himself. With a wistful smile, he turned and began walking towards his room, in one of the bylanes above a clothes shop.

'Namaste, Vini Bhai!' He saw a familiar group of old men, sitting on charpoys and sipping hot tea. 'Come. There's hot ginger chai. Your favourite.'

'Namaste, namaste!' Vini plonked himself on a vacant charpoy. He took a glass of steaming hot tea from his friend and took a long sip. 'Ahh! That's just what I needed! Haven't had *adrakh wali* chai for a week! You don't know how terrible it is to have tea bags and boiled water!'

One of the men pointed at his ektara bag and asked him, 'Where did you go this time?' The men would wait for Vini to get back from his foreign trips. They wanted to be the first to know of his adventures and listened to him with rapt attention. Often, younger people joined them and sat huddled around the rickety charpoys, wrapped in frayed blankets on cold, wintry mornings.

Vini would often break into song spontaneously as he shared the stories. And that day was no different.

Vini told them about Prague. He talked of the ancient city as if it were a magical, faraway land. He told them of the enchanting astronomical clock face, and the otherworldly feeling one got standing on the famous Charles Bridge. The old men listened, fascinated. He then told them of the great crusades that had been fought in that land, and they held their breath, wide-eyed. Eventually, Vini broke the spell. He pulled out his phone and began showing them pictures of the concert and the places he had just described.

Nearly an hour had gone by without anyone noticing. The sun had risen, and soon, the place would begin to get crowded. One of the men asked Vini to sing something for them before he went to his room. Vini nodded, tenderly took his ektara out of its cover and sang a song by the maverick poet Meeraji.

'Nagri nagri phiraa musaafir
ghar kaa rastaa bhuul gayaa
Kyaa hai teraa kyaa hai meraa
apnaa paraayaa bhuul gayaa
Yaad ke pher mein aa kar dil par
aisi kaari chot lagi
Dukh mein sukh hai sukh mein dukh hai
bhed ye nyaaraa bhuul gayaa'

Vini explained,

'Many cities the wanderer roamed
and forgot his way back home.
What is yours, what is mine,
he forgot who is friend or foe.
Caught in a vicious cycle of memories,
his heart was mercilessly hurt.
Joy resides in sadness, and grief hides in pleasure,
he forgot this profound secret . . .'

'Vini Bhai, you must tell our youngsters about your travels. You are really lucky. We will never get a chance to go to those foreign lands,' one of the friends said with a sigh.

'Yes, Vini, you have so many stories to tell. Your own life must be so fascinating. You hardly talk about yourself.'

'There's nothing much to share, brothers. You all know everything about me. This man in front of you is an open book.' Vini laughed.

'No. You must tell us more about your life. You are a mysterious man, *bhai*,' one of the men insisted.

Vini became quiet. He hardly spoke about his past to anyone. But he never hid anything when he was questioned directly. People tend to probe into things that are denied to them. If you avoid talking about something, they want to know the reason and eventually, the truth, however uninteresting, does come out.

'Okay, my friends. But it's a long story. So let's sit in the evening. Right now, I need to have a wash and rest a bit,' said Vini.

'Oh, yes, yes! So sorry! We forgot that you've just returned from a long journey. Let's meet for chai in the evening,' the man said.

Vini agreed and began walking towards his room.

'Namaste, Binny Uncleji!' Monu greeted Vini loudly. Monu was a plump young man with the mannerisms of a twelve-year-old. He was driving a noisy Rajdoot motorcycle with large aluminium canisters hanging on either side, in which he supplied fresh milk. 'Can I drop you home?' Monu offered.

Although his home was hardly 200 metres away, Vini didn't refuse the good natured Monu. He got on to the bike with difficulty, since he had to hold both his bags up in the air as he clambered on. His thigh muscle cramped as he adjusted himself on the frayed, wide seat, wedged between the milk cans. Monu insisted that Vini rest the bags on the cans.

As they travelled on the bumpy dirt lane, Monu asked, 'Where are you coming from, Uncleji?' Vini said he was returning from Europe. 'Don't you have luggage?' Monu sounded surprised.

Vini asked him, 'What about your luggage?'

Monu laughed. He lived right there and was just selling milk on his motorbike. 'Why would I have luggage, Uncleji? You only carry luggage when you travel!'

Vini smiled and said, 'Isn't everyone travelling in this world?'

Monu guffawed innocently as he brought the bike to a halt in front of Vini's room. 'You are such a funny man, Uncleji. I really like to be with you.'

Vini smiled at Monu's simplicity. He was so pure. Why couldn't more people be like him? 'You must have travelled to a lot of places,' Monu said. 'Do take me with you some time. I want to see the world too!'

Vini nodded. 'Of course, Monu. We will surely go on a journey together. Thank you so much for the ride.'

'Namaste Uncleji,' Monu said and drove off happily.

That evening, true to his promise, Vini came to the *majlis*. It was Vini who had given the name 'majlis' to the gathering. He had encountered the tradition in Bengal. The Arabic word 'majlis' means a council or a place where people gather for news, catching up and storytelling. The name had brought a sense of dignity to the daily gatherings, discouraging loose talk and gossip.

'Let me tell you about a man I knew once, long ago,' Vini began. 'His name is . . . was Ashwini.' The majlis was all ears now.

Vini continued, 'This Ashwini Kumar Singh was a very nasty man. He had harmed many people. From a young age, he had become a con man. By the time he turned thirty-one, he was stinking rich. He'd hoodwinked innocent people and stolen their hard-earned money. He had everything, but he wasn't satisfied. He wanted more. Ashwini had authored three bestselling books, which were quite popular among youngsters. He had paid needy writers paltry sums to write these books. He was a good orator and was often invited to speak on various platforms. He had an affable public image. Ashwini was an expert at hiding his nasty nature in public.

'Ashwini was from Dhanbad, the land of black gold. He had been an extremely bright boy. And he was very, very ambitious. He had grown up in the streets of Dhanbad. He was frustrated there. He wanted to get rich quickly, and there was nothing he could do in the small town. He dreamt of having big cars, a palatial house, liveried servants and so much money that he could light a cigarette with a hundred-rupee note fifty times a day! He'd seen a movie where a gangster did just that.

'He went for his higher studies to Calcutta and never returned to Dhanbad . . .'

Vini paused and took a long, deep breath. 'When a man is desperate to get rich quickly, he is bound to look for short cuts. And such short cuts, more often than not, take the unscrupulous route. In Calcutta, Ashwini soon found the way to make quick money. He was smart and ready to break the rules if he was paid good money. Thus, he rapidly cultivated a sizeable number of dubious contacts, who helped him to get rich quickly.

'Ashwini had made a big part of his fortune by supplying stolen coal. He had started off by handling part of a racket where mines that didn't exist on ground were shown, on paper, as coal-producing. These fictitious mines were owned by political bigwigs who had their goons steal coal from goods trains or *maal gaadis*. The stolen coal was shown as mined from their non-existent mines, and sold off to dubious and illegal outfits. Ashwini had a brilliant mind and soon started getting noticed by the gang lords. The work was very dangerous, and there were regular gang wars for the stolen coal. After a terrible shootout, Ashwini escaped by the skin of his teeth, hidden under a heap of coal on a maal gaadi, and reached Bombay with his pregnant wife, Pratima.'

Vini had a distant look in his eyes as he went silent. The majlis sat in rapt attention. 'What happened in Bombay?' someone asked.

Vini jerked back to reality. 'Ah, yes, Bombay. The city of dreams . . . Ashwini began to set up a business empire in Bombay with the money he had made. He was extremely aggressive, ruthless and violent. His wife, Pratima, was emotionally distant and scared of his temper. She had nowhere to go. They had twin daughters, who weren't comfortable in his presence. As they started growing up, they began to lie to get whatever they wanted. It was the only trait they seemed to have picked up from their father. Ashwini often slapped the girls, and sometimes he even hit Pratima, when he caught the girls lying to him. He blamed her for everything the girls did and didn't do. Pratima was terrified of Ashwini. She was desperately looking for a way to escape the loveless, abusive marriage that she was stuck in.

'Ashwini had two cousins who had reached Bombay from Dhanbad, looking for better opportunities. The men weren't educated. They were god-fearing and not dishonest. They thoroughly disliked Ashwini, but since they needed his help, they had to be polite to his face, and Ashwini knew this. He enjoyed sneering at them and treated them like dirt. He insulted them at every possible opportunity.

'It was pretty obvious that Ashwini had no real friends, but a large number of sycophants hovered around him because of his money and the power he wielded. Ashwini enjoyed playing god; or, more appropriately, the devil. His staff were mortified by his unpredictable moods and temper. No one knew what would annoy the boss and who was going to have their last day at work when they stood before him. Ashwini's language was peppered with abusive and aggressive phrases. He had developed a knack for identifying and employing weak-minded and needy people, who constantly took his oppression lying down.

'On the other hand, Ashwini himself was ready to grovel to the lowest clerk in a government office when he had to get a deal approved. He could sweet-talk his way in and out of most situations. But, as is the wont of such men, Ashwini was extremely vindictive. He remembered every slight and cold shoulder, and made sure that, when the time came, which it always did, each such instance was suitably "repaid".

'Ashwini was known as Ash or AK to the people who were informal with him. It goes without saying that Ash was not above offering bribes to get off the hook after breaking the law, and that he sneered at law enforcers. Many a time, when he was with his drinking partners—who were with him only for the lavish partying—he would show off by deliberately jumping red lights in one of his Mercs, Jaguars or Rolls-Royces, so that he would get pulled over by cops. Then, he would bribe them by tossing money at them. If a cop turned out to be honest and refused to be bought, a call would be made to someone higher up who was more "agreeable" and a bigger bribe would be paid, and soon all would be well in Ash's world. "Everyone can be bought," Ash would proudly boast. "If someone has their morals screwed on too tight, then their bosses can be bought. All you need are the right contacts and loads of money."

'Ash's ruthlessness was well known. Over the previous few years, he had become the idol of a lot of IIM graduates. Many of these young men loved his brash and brazen bad-boy image. In fact, a sizeable number wanted to live up to that image. They saw

Ash's money-making and spending styles—just the stuff of their dreams. Another set of starry-eyed fans saw him as the man who would transform India's economic woes.

'Ash had a powerful PR machinery in place, and it ensured Ash's public image was constantly scrubbed and kept spotlessly clean. Political parties came and went, but people like Ash inevitably sailed through, unscathed. In the ten years he'd spent in Bombay, Ash had managed to add an astounding number of powerful people on his speed-dial list.

'The year Ash entered his fourth decade was special. He had decided to back a powerful political party in the forthcoming elections. This move had come after he snubbed a smaller party that he had supported earlier. With many politicians, police officers and municipal corporators in his pocket, Ash had rapidly become the epitome of decadence and corruption,' Vini concluded.

'Vini Bhai, we asked you to tell us your story, but you are telling us the story of some other man,' one of the friends spoke up.

'This *is* my story, dear friend.' Vini smiled.

'Can't be. This man is really nasty and terrible. And he has a lot of money. This cannot be you.'

Vini looked amused and shrugged. 'Then why don't you listen to it as the story of this nasty and terrible man?'

'That's not such a bad idea. The story sounds good. Please tell us more about Ashwini. He sounds like he needs to be thrashed!' a majlis friend commented.

'Absolutely,' another friend added. 'And, he will soon be straightened out, I hope.'

'Yes,' continued Vini. 'It is a universal truth that when family and friends do not straighten out a crooked person, the whole world thrashes them much worse. And that was what was to happen to Ashwini. But that happens much later in the story. So, would you like me to continue Ashwini's tale?'

'Yes, please do, Vini. We all know that there's always something interesting at the end of each of your stories,' one friend said.

'Yes. But you all will have to wait a while till we get to the end of Ashwini's tale. Okay, so let me tell you how Ashwini's fall began,' Vini said.

'Ash had made so many enemies along the way that it is difficult to say when it really was the beginning of his end. But, dear friends, time has a great way of levelling things, and Ash was on the brink. His *paap ka ghada*, the pot of sins, was full.

'The political party he had snubbed was waiting for the right opportunity to destroy him. The competitors he had finished off, when he used his powerful contacts to get lucrative contracts, were gunning for him. The Anti-Corruption Bureau was constantly sniffing at his heels. The Crime Branch was trying to link him with underworld gangsters and the drug mafia. Envious industrialists had their spies snooping around, and hard-nosed, scoop-seeking journalists were on to him, seeking to finish off his public career. And, to top it all, his own wife was looking for a reason to get out of their marriage.'

Vini let out a long sigh. 'But ironically, it was none of these big cannons that triggered his downslide. Ashwini's nemesis was a lone gate-crasher on a death wish.'

2

Young Man in a Hurry

'Have landed. See you in ten,' Jay texted Pam, his partner.

Paramjeet Sikka, or Pam, was one of the three partners who, along with Jay, had started ALSOL three years ago. Pam had been in college with Jay. She was a banker who had reluctantly left her job in Singapore to raise her twins. A couple of years down the line, with the kids going to school now, Pam had begun itching to take up work that gave her enough time for the family. When Jay had asked her to join him at ALSOL, she had jumped at the opportunity.

The other two partners were Shyam Beniwal and Girish Chander, who were only interested in the profit ALSOL was making. Shyam was in his forties. His family owned a couple of jewellery stores. Jay's father had often told Jay to be wary of him. Jay made no bones about the fact that Shyam was his primary investor and scoffed at his dad's misgivings. The fourth partner, Girish, was clear that he was in this venture only for the money. He was a real-estate agent and had parked his black money in ALSOL. Both Shyam and Girish were happy to let Jay and Pam run ALSOL. Each of the four held 25 per cent share in the company and had made a tidy sum in the past two years.

ALSOL, or Alpha Line Solutions, had had a meteoric rise. From a small turnkey solutions company running out of Jay's dad's garage, ALSOL had become a success story within three years. Jay spearheaded operations, and his aggressive style had shades of ruthlessness that had gained him a number of enemies. Jay was quite proud of this. He believed that though many people can have powerful friends, only successful people have powerful enemies.

Jay rushed out of the airport to the Audi Q7. Pam was waiting for him impatiently. 'Ouch. Damn!' Jay exclaimed as he bumped his head while leaping into the SUV.

'And a very good afternoon to you too. You're losing your style, Jay.' Pam grinned.

'Hey, Pam! Can't help being tall and handsome, you know! Hey boss, *aaraam se*!' He cursed again as their vehicle lurched forward, and then stopped almost immediately when their driver had to slam the brakes. A car in front of them had screeched to a halt. The car behind them honked loudly and nearly banged into them.

'What's the problem with everyone nowadays? People have no patience at all. Unbelievable, man!' Jay shook his head looking at the mad traffic outside Delhi airport and let out an incredulous laugh. He didn't want to let road rage spoil his mood today. The driver was paid for that. He chuckled as he turned slightly to face Pam. 'Style is as style does, Pam, and today, our style got us this!' He pulled out an envelope from his suit's inner breast pocket with a flourish. It was the document the industrialist had signed a few hours ago at the Mumbai airport. 'YES! I did it, Pam! Woohoo!'

Pam laughed seeing the look on Jay's face. 'You look like you just scored with your high school crush!'

'This feels a hundred times better, Pam! Now, let's meet this Hooda and seal the second deal for the day!' Jay laughed.

'How can you be sure?'

'Well, since he's meeting us in a hotel, and not at his office, it means that he wants this to be discreet, which in my language means that, with the right amount of grease, the wheels will turn smoothly.' Jay faced Pam squarely, his eyes shining. 'I will make a 10k bet with you Pam, that Surinder Sharma will also be there. They are all in this together.'

'No bets. I always lose bets with you. But who's he?'

'The officer who will sanction the contract.'

'I doubt it. But I guess you know how this game is played better than anyone else.'

Jay chuckled.

They made it through the mind-numbing traffic to the Carousel by the skin of their teeth, reaching at 4.28 p.m. Ranjit Hooda, the sports minister's wife's second cousin, was already there. Sagar was waiting for them, pacing anxiously at the reception. He ushered them into a sprawling double suite on the fourth floor of the hotel.

Hooda was sitting on a plush brown sofa, looking bored. He was in his trademark beige safari suit. On wooden chairs opposite him, across a low glass table, sat two men looking earnest and nervous, talking quickly and over each other. Hooda glanced at Sagar, who wordlessly conveyed that Jay and Pam had arrived by jerking his chin towards them. Hooda nodded silently and turned back to the two men who were animatedly trying to explain something to him. They seemed to have realized that the guy wasn't too keen to hear them out. Hooda raised his palm, indicating that they should stop.

'I really don't think this is a good idea. You both meet Sagar. He will explain what I want.'

The men got the hint, gulped and fell silent. They glanced at each other, nodded and quickly got up. Staring at Jay and Pam, they shuffled out of the room.

'Ahh! Mr Jayshankar! Come, come. Sit down. Sagar, please organize tea for everyone. Did you brief Mr Jayshankar?' Sagar shook his head. Hooda frowned instantly before turning to face Jay.

Jay shook Hooda's sweaty palm and introduced Pam. Hooda didn't shake her hand but did a namaste as everyone sat down. He took a long breath and began. 'Look, Mr Jayshankar. This is a very important project for our minister. I am sure you are aware that there are many more projects you can do for us.' He trailed off as he glanced at Sagar.

Jay watched a rapid, unspoken exchange happening between them. Hooda was attempting to communicate something but didn't want to say it aloud. Jay smiled inwardly. He knew what he had to say. 'You please do not worry at all, sir. I know that the elections are coming, and there are important arrangements to be made. We are there to take care of everything, sir. I will discuss the details with Sagar.'

Hooda relaxed and let out a breath, visibly relieved.

'Call me Jay, please.'

'Aah! Good. Jay it is, then. You all can discuss the details.' He turned to Sagar. 'What do you think, Sagar?'

'Project cost allocation is 250 crore, sir. The park has to be made quickly, as panchayat elections are coming up. Minister Saheb must inaugurate it before the monsoon.'

'Why so?'

Jay had caught on. 'Sir, renovation will need to be done after the rains. Painting, cement work, landscaping, etc. Project estimate will be 7.5 crore. I will get it done in five. Rest is yours. This is possible twice a year, around Holi and Diwali.'

'You are a smart man, Mr Jayshankar. Jay.' Hooda chuckled.

Sagar looked impressed. Jay was ensuring a regular income for everyone.

'Twenty-five?' Hooda looked at Jay hopefully.

Jay shook his head. 'Too much.' He consciously didn't add the obligatory 'sir'. Now he had them, and he had done his homework well. Hooda was desperate. The coalition government was on a sticky wicket, and Hooda's brother-in-law's political bosses weren't too happy with him. This guy needed this sham project to begin immediately, so that he could use the funds to grease palms and win the panchayat elections. No one would care about what happened to the amusement park once it was inaugurated. Except when it was repaired and renovated, twice a year.

'Eight,' Jay said shortly.

Pam was watching this exchange with trepidation. She had the good sense to keep quiet and knew that Jay would manage it. He was a master at this.

Sagar interjected, 'We can look at fifteen.' Hooda was looking a bit nervous now.

Jay shook his head firmly. He wasn't looking at them but staring at a beautifully framed painting of flowers in a vase on the wall behind Hooda. He knew this was the make-or-break moment.

Pam had her teeth clenched. Her fists were balled up under her thighs. She held her breath.

'We can do ten and no more. Otherwise we will have to call it off. Sir.' Jay spoke in measured tones, almost in a whisper.

Hooda began drumming the fingers of his right hand on the sofa arm. It was something he did unconsciously when he was stressed. He began frowning as he locked eyes with Sagar. Jay ignored the urge to look at them exchanging glances. He kept staring at the painting. He noted that the wooden frame looked a bit too perfect, and then he realized that it was faux wood, made to look like the real thing. Everything was like this frame nowadays, he thought. Made to look like the real deal, and yet, a total sham. Like this amusement park project.

The silence, punctuated by Hooda's drumming, was deafening.

Hooda came to a decision and picked up the receiver of the intercom on a small side table to his right. 'Please send Mr Sharma inside.'

No words were exchanged, and each second seemed like an hour to Pam. She followed Jay's gaze and looked at the painting, not really able to understand what his game plan was.

A knock, and the door opened. A lanky, bespectacled man with a thin moustache walked in. Jay glanced at him before his eyes met Pam's. Jay raised an eyebrow slightly, as if saying to her, 'What did I tell you?' Then he gave her a quick, jubilant wink. Pam looked at him admiringly.

The cut-off date was also an obvious sham, and Sharma, the sanctioning officer, was surely going to make a big profit out of this, courtesy of ALSOL.

'Sharma, this is Mr Jayshankar. His company ALSOL will be handling the project. Sagar will handle the details. Now I have to rush.' Hooda got up with uncharacteristic energy, belying his huge frame. 'Sorry, but I have a guitar class in ten minutes. Sagar, please give them tea before they leave. Good day, Jay.' Quickly shaking Jay's hand, he rushed out.

Everything after that was a blur. Jay had zoned out. He'd clinched the deal.

The required papers were in a file in front of Jay. Pam saw Jay's faraway look, grabbed the file and handed it to Sagar with trembling hands. Her heart was thumping as Sharma signed them hurriedly.

'Sagar, keep the originals with you and give them a copy when they bring the donation.' Sharma looked up at Jay. 'Get the cash within three days, or this is null and void,' he growled as he rushed after Hooda.

Jay nodded carelessly. He wanted to get away from this place.

Soon, they were back in the Audi. Pam was speaking to Girish, their partner. 'Girish, we did it! Jay was brilliant, as usual. Along with a recurring half-yearly repair job. Hooda wanted twenty-five. Jay got it done in ten! That slimeball Sharma was there too. Can you beat it? These guys don't have any scruples at all! Luckily, neither do we!'

Pam watched Jay as she spoke. He sat silently, looking out of the darkened window. The car was going around India Gate. His phone was buzzing repeatedly in his jacket pocket, but he ignored it. His face was expressionless. She could make out that he was far away, in some daydream. She let him be.

The train is within his reach. He is running really fast now. The platform begins to extend below his feet as he races towards the train.

Pam's phone buzzed, and she saw that it was Shyam, their fourth partner, calling from Paris. It was always tough talking to him. She was intimidated by Shyam. She answered the call in almost a whisper. Shyam spoke in measured tones. He wanted to congratulate Jay. 'Jay . . .'

The hands grasping at him are receding. The train seems to hold its speed constant and doesn't accelerate any further. It seems to be alive. It has sensed Jay's desperation . . .

'Jay . . .'

He is running pretty fast now. The gap between him and the bogies is gradually reducing. 'Get in, get in! Get in, get in!' the couplings seemed to say to him rhythmically. He crouches slightly as he hurtles ahead, about to take a leap, just as he passes the last bogie . . .

'Uh-huh?!' Jay jerked back into the car. He had dozed off. It had been a long day.

'It's Shyam. From Paris.'

Jay took the phone. 'Hi,' he mumbled. Pleasantries were exchanged. Shyam was concerned that their tax liability would include the tax on the Rs 10-crore bribe. Also, who knew what would happen in case the government fell. Jay was a bit irritated.

'Shyam, we just got the deal. Don't worry. I've managed this. I will manage that too . . . *Bhai*, we'll cross that bridge when we get to it. Right now, you just enjoy your holiday. And, get back safely.'

Jay looked thoroughly cheesed off and shook his head as he tossed the phone back to Pam. 'Sometimes he's too much! He should be celebrating, but he's thinking of tax and losses. We are still going to make fifteen crore on this, yaar. Even after paying the tax on Hooda's booty, we will get around three crore each, dammit!' Jay was frowning. He looked at his watch. It was nearly three o'clock. 'Drop me off at Dad's.'

Pam sighed. She knew how Jay's moods fluctuated. Now wasn't a time to say anything. She instructed her driver to take them via Defence Colony, where Jay's parents lived. Jay sat sullen-faced, staring into space. Pam dove into her phone.

They arrived at his place in fifteen minutes. 'Don't spoil your mood for him, Jay. You know Shyam only means well for all of us,' Pam said as Jay opened the door to get out of the car. She reached out, patted him on his shoulder and hugged him.

Jay forced a smile and nodded. 'Yes. Sometimes I just can't stand him. But he's a good guy, Pam. He's never let me down. We'll celebrate once he's back.'

'You did good today.' Pam smiled as the car drove off.

Jay grinned and gave a passing salute as he waved goodbye to her. He then turned around to enter his childhood home.

3

The Gatecrasher

When the majlis gathered the next day, many more people had joined in. Most were keen to hear Vini speak about Ash, but some of them knew that the reticent man talking to them had helped many transform their lives. Vini had a wealth of wisdom, but he wouldn't speak on his own. He had to be 'strummed' like his ektara.

'Talk to us of pride,' said the oldest member of the majlis.

'Pride, or egotism, is *haumai*,' Vini smiled softly as he commenced the majlis once again.

> *'Naanak haumai rog bure,*
> *Je dekhaan te ekaa bedhan*
> *aape bakhsai sabad dhure.*
> *Aape parkhe parakhnahaarai*
> *bahur soolaak na hoiee*
> *Jin kau nadhar bhiee gur mele*
> *prabh bhaanaa sach soiee.'*

'Nanak, the sickness of egotism is truly dangerous.

Everywhere I see the same pain,
He Himself bestows His word.
When He tests a mortal Himself,
one is never judged again.
Those fortunate to have attained the Guru,
are ones who realize God.'

Vini continued, 'Pride is a dangerous thing, my dear friends. Let me share a story with you all before we go on.

'Once, a rat entered a jewellery shop and swallowed a large diamond worth crores. An employee had seen the rat scurrying in the tray where the diamonds were kept and concluded that it was the culprit. He chased the rat but couldn't catch it. The rat quickly disappeared into the street outside.

'The owner panicked and began organizing search parties, but to no avail. He then announced a large prize for anyone who could catch the rat and retrieve the diamond. In a couple of days, someone located the rat's nest beneath the jewellery shop. There were hundreds of rats there, and all of them looked alike!

'Many hapless rats were caught, but the diamond swallower couldn't be located. The owner was at his wits' end. Finally, one man went into the rat nest and caught the elusive rat in a single visit.

'The owner was elated. He asked the man how he found the rat so easily when everyone else had tried so hard and failed. The man said, "Rats are no different from men. Of all the rats, this was the only one who sat aloof, on a high pedestal, preening itself."'

'Dear friends,' Vini said to the majlis, 'pride makes us believe we are special and important, and we forget that everything that has been bestowed upon us can also be taken away in a single moment.'

* * *

Ash was like the rat that had swallowed a priceless diamond. He lived a lavish lifestyle and enjoyed flaunting his wealth. On his thirty-second birthday, Ash threw a grand party at JW Marriott, and the who's who of the city were in attendance. The menu was unending, the ambience was excellent and wine flowed like water.

A couple of well-known Bollywood singers were regaling everyone with the latest hits and soon, everyone was on the dance floor. Ash loved singing and was pulled up on stage to sing with the stars. He was having a grand time. Soon after, a popular DJ began belting out blaring trance music as the lights dimmed and smoke machines began spewing clouds of thick white steam. Strobes and laser lights matched the rhythm of the music, reflecting blinding and colourful flashes off the large disco ball spinning above the floor. Ash was dancing on the crowded floor with his wife, Pratima, and the party was in full swing.

All of a sudden, a bedraggled man came up through the thick smoke. 'Ashwini!' He shouted, but he couldn't be heard over the music. He grabbed Ash's shoulder and tried to pull Ash towards himself. 'Hey, Ashwini!'

the man said loudly. Ash wasn't sure who the man was and thought he was someone who had come to wish him. He turned, smiling and shaking his head to the music. The man shouted over the music into Ash's ear, 'Ashwini Kumar Singh, do you remember me at all? Haah! How could you! You only remember people who you need something from!'

Ash frowned slightly. He dimly remembered the man as an old colleague and competitor, whom Ash had betrayed right at the beginning of his dubious career in Bombay. He ignored the barb and feigned having forgotten the man. Then he said, 'Oh! Hi! So sorry I didn't recognize you. You have changed so much! Please enjoy the party, my friend!' He turned back to his wife, rolled his eyes and began to dance again. Pratima looked concerned as the man continued to heckle Ash.

The man wouldn't let Ash go. He rasped, 'All good things come to an end, Mr Ashwini, and your debacle is coming soon.'

Ash was getting thoroughly fed up with the man and tried to get away, pulling Pratima along. The man kept following them through the swaying dancers. As Ash snaked through the crowd, everyone wanted to wish him, and he was constantly stopped on the crowded dance floor. No one noticed when the heckler put a crumpled piece of paper into Ash's suit pocket. He then grabbed Ash's arm, stuck his face right in front of Ash's and swallowed a tablet, staring into Ash's eyes as he spoke in a grating voice,

'*Jab naash manuj par chhaataa hai,*
pehle vivek mar jaataa hai.
Hitavachan nahin toone maanaa,
maitri ka moolya na pehchaanaa,
To le, main bhi ab jaataa hoon,
antim sankalp sunaataa hoon.
Yaachanaa nahin, ab rann hoga,
jeevan-jai yaa ki marann hoga!'

Vini elaborated,

'When calamity engulfs man,
discerning right from wrong is first to die.
You neither agreed to good counsel,
nor did you recognize the value of friendship.
Note this, now I too shall depart,
announcing my final decision.
There won't be any further pleadings;
it will be war, life's victory or death it shall be!'

The man's vice-like grip on Ash's arm began to loosen. He stood in front of Ash for a few seconds as his mouth began to froth and his eyes began to glaze over. Then, he teetered and swayed with the music blaring on. By now Ash had wrested his arm out of the man's hold and turned away. But he turned back almost immediately, realizing that the man had fallen on him. He saw the man drop to the floor with a thud. The man had collapsed. He writhed and shuddered, until his body stopped moving. The people in the immediate vicinity thought he'd had a drink too many. They moved slightly away from him and continued dancing to the music. Someone called out to a waiter, and the hotel staff called security immediately.

Aghast, Ash stood and watched as security guards dragged the unconscious man off the dance floor, apologizing for the gate-crasher. Ash's vindictive temperament surfaced moments later, when he turned to Pratima and hissed, 'I will destroy that stupid man. How dare he come here and spoil my party! I will get him thrown in jail and have him thrashed all day and night for a month.' His wife looked troubled but kept quiet, as always.

Ash started dancing again. He didn't want his party to be remembered as a dud. But things were just getting started.

A few minutes later, the security chief of the hotel came rushing to find Ash. He whispered into Ash's ear that the man was dead. He had apparently consumed a cyanide capsule. An ambulance was on the way. A duty constable was waiting outside with the body until the police van arrived. Ash walked off the dance floor, stunned. He instructed the organizers not to inform anyone of this. He went outside and gave his statement to the constable that the gate-crasher was not known to anyone in his party. Then, he called his PR guys and instructed them to ensure that the incident wasn't connected to him or his birthday party by the press in any way. In fact, it would be best if it were kept out of the press completely.

When Ash re-entered the party it was still in full swing. No one had realized that he had been missing for nearly thirty minutes. He wanted to shake off the uncomfortable feeling. He realized that he had beads of cold sweat on his forehead and reached into his suit pocket for his handkerchief. His fingers felt the folded piece of paper. He pulled out and unfolded the lined sheet. It was a single-page, handwritten letter. He realized with shock that it was from the dead man. He quickly folded and stuffed it back into his pocket. He strode along the edge of the dance floor, looking for a secluded place, and sat down in an empty corner. His guests, oblivious of what had happened, kept dancing to the deafening music.

Ash now opened the note and read it in the rhythmically flashing blue strobe light from the dance floor. The man had accused Ash for the circumstances leading to his suicide, and the note ended with the same verses that he had spouted just before his death. These were lines that Ash knew well from his childhood. They were from a popular portion of the poem 'Rashmirathi'.

Wide-eyed, Ash crumpled the note and threw it towards a garbage bin. It hit the edge of the bin and fell on the floor. He sat staring at the dance floor. He had gone completely numb. His eyes were losing focus. He could only hear the thumping music, and his heartbeat began to synchronize with it. He couldn't breathe freely and wanted to get up and run outside. But it was his own party, and he had a lot at stake. He had to be *seen* with the who's who of the city. Ash started taking deep breaths and composed himself. He got up and walked back to the party. He didn't mention anything to anyone, especially his wife. Pratima realized that something wasn't right. But was anything ever right in Ash's world? She knew better than to question him and decided to let sleeping dogs lie.

Ash tried to keep his composure and made light of the gate-crasher, but the dead man's words kept bombarding him. He forced his face into a smile and continued partying far into the night.

It was past 1 a.m. when Ash and Pratima saw their last guests off. Ash looked weary and preoccupied, and Pratima shrugged it off as the effect of a long day. Ash was restless. Pratima watched him looking back into the hotel repeatedly as they stood waiting for their car to arrive. Just as their chauffeur drove in to pick them up, Ash suddenly turned and ran back inside. Pratima was surprised, but she sat in the car quietly. She had learnt long ago not to ask Ash any questions.

Ash ran all the way back inside, to where he had sat down and read the dead man's note. The hotel staff were busy cleaning the party hall. Chairs and tables had already been removed and were being stacked one on top of another by two sleepy and bored-looking men. Ash reached the general spot where he had sat while reading the letter. He looked around wildly, trying to reorient himself as he tried to remember the direction in which he had tossed the confounded ball of paper. He scanned the carpeted floor and saw a crumpled white paper. He leaped to grab it, only to realize that it was a napkin. He peered under the stacked tables and chairs. The staff watched him curiously. One of them came up to ask if he had lost something and needed any help. Ash quickly waved him off. Finally, he found the letter lying crumpled next to a pillar. He snatched it up and smoothed it out to confirm before letting out a cry of jubilation.

By then, nearly fifteen minutes had gone by, and Pratima had finally decided to come looking for him. Seeing her, Ash quickly put the letter into his pocket once more and strode outside, without explaining anything. She almost had to jog to catch up with him.

Ash didn't speak to Pratima throughout the drive back home. She didn't want to rock the boat either. They reached home at 1.45 a.m., and without saying a word, he went off to his own bedroom, where he slept alone. Pratima didn't appear to exist for him. She, too, walked towards her room quickly. She hardly cared any more.

Ash quickly got out of his suit and tossed it over a chair. He rushed into the bathroom and washed his face, desperately trying to get rid of the terrible thoughts that were raging inside his head. He looked at the ashen face staring back at him in the mirror. He seemed to have aged a decade that night. He got in bed but sleep refused to arrive. He tossed and turned, playing the entire sequence in his head, over and over. The dead man's face kept flashing in front of him. Ash could not forget the man's eyes. Each time Ash closed his eyes, the man stared back at him, repeating the ominous lines,

'Jab naash manuj par chhaataa hai,
pehle vivek mar jaataa hai.'

Ash had never been so rattled in all his life. The closest he had felt to this was when, as a student, he had seen a man being lynched on the streets of Calcutta. He had watched the terrible scene with morbid fascination from his hostel window, and that image had remained with him for a long time. There was no remorse in him for not trying to save that man. In fact, Ash never ever helped anyone in need. A person had to be useful to further Ash's ambitions or their existence didn't matter to him.

But tonight's incident was different. This man had committed suicide right in front of him, and he had accused Ash for driving him to that point. He had left the suicide note that Ash had with him. *That note!* Thank god he had been able to retrieve it before someone else could get their hands on it!

Ash was wide awake by now and leaped out of bed. How had he forgotten to take the crumpled note out of his suit pocket? He needed to destroy that incriminating piece of evidence immediately. It would completely finish him, if it got into the wrong hands.

He looked at the clock. It was 4.05 a.m. It took him a minute to recollect where he had tossed his suit, and in the semi-darkness he plunged his hand into the suit pocket, seeking to grab the crumpled ball of his *entire existence*.

Vini sighed as he said the last two words and stopped.

* * *

The majlis sat in silence. One could have heard a pin drop. From afar, a factory siren began wailing as it signalled the end of a long and weary day.

Vini smiled wistfully at the appropriateness of the wailing siren. The sun would set soon, and the world would go to sleep, only to awaken to another long day. He resumed softly, 'Yes, that's all Ash was in that moment, a crumpled ball of nastiness and ruthless ambition. He had no one to turn to. He was at the nadir of his pathetic existence. He had been beaten by one unassailable man who had won by swallowing a cyanide capsule.

To le, main bhi ab jaataa hoon,
antim sankalp sunaataa hoon.

'Dawn filtered through long French windows as Ash held his crumpled life in his hand. He smoothed the paper to read the letter a third time. His eyes widened as he saw the words glowing softly with a golden fire. His mind was playing tricks upon him, he knew. He shook his head, blinked his eyes a few times and sat on his bed, holding what appeared to be his own epitaph in his hands.

'As he slowly read the letter once again, he could hear the man's ominous voice in his head.

Yaachanaa nahin, ab rann hoga,
jeevan-jai yaa ki marann hoga!'

Vini sat quietly, looking into infinity. Suddenly, he looked tired. Everyone listening to him had become quiescent and pensive. The sun had set, and from afar, the sounds of traffic and the bustling crowd around the mall floated up to them in the soft breeze.

'I would like to go and rest. I think it's the jet lag creeping up. Let's continue tomorrow,' he said softly, and the majlis broke up without a word.

4

Family and a Friend

Jay's parents' home, in A Block, Defence Colony, was a two-storey house that had been built by Jay's grandfather, who had served in the Indian Army. Jay's father, Satish, was still an infant when the family had settled there. Jay had also lived there all his life, until recently, when he had taken up an apartment at Hauz Khas with his girlfriend, Ritika.

The metal gate was rusty and made a loud squeaking sound as Jay pushed it open. He shook his head as he heard the irritating high-pitched noise. His mother refused to have it oiled. She said it alerted her to anyone coming or going.

As Jay walked in, he saw that the lawn to his left had just been watered and there was water on the sandstone slabs that lined the walkway. He gingerly stepped over the first puddle, trying not to wet his brogues, and then, something came over him. He took a little hop and landed into the next puddle with a splash, wetting the shoe. He skipped the next one, determinedly, feeling the squelch of sun-warmed water around his foot. For the next puddle, which was a bit far, he needed to crouch slightly to get traction. 'Hop, skip and . . .' he took the leap, 'jump!' he grunted as he landed right in the middle of the puddle, making a large splash. He grinned to himself as he felt the warm water seep into the other shoe.

'You've not done that in years. You used to do that every day when you got back from school,' laughed Jay's mother, Shubhra, who stood on the porch next to the lawn. Two steps led up to it. There was a small settee and two cane chairs, with worn and faded cushions, on the porch, which had a metal grill running all around it.

Jay grinned.

'And then, you would walk inside in your wet shoes, leaving the drawing-room carpet soggy. And I would shout,' said Shubhra with a chuckle.

Jay's dad, Satish, who had followed her out, said, 'Then, you stomped your feet again and again to tease her!'

'Dad, Ma, I just cracked the deal!' Jay spoke excitedly as he came up the steps, kicking off the wet shoes and socks.

'Congratulations, béta!' Shubhra smiled as they went in. Satish simply said, 'Very good, Jay.' He was a man of few words. Shubhra chattered on, about what she had cooked that day and about some friends who had come over and were inquiring about Jay. Jay wasn't really listening. He saw that his dad had a serious expression on his face. Turning away from his mom, he looked directly at his dad and asked, 'Aren't you happy for me, Dad?'

'Of course I am, Jay. I just congratulated you.'

'You don't *look* happy.' Jay frowned slightly.

Satish sighed and sat down, looking at the floor, avoiding Jay's stare. 'Jay, you know me. I worry for you. You are going too fast. I have always believed in taking things slow.'

Jay could feel the hair on his nape bristling. His face darkened. Shubhra could read the familiar signs of an unpleasant fight coming on. She got up quickly. She knew she had about five minutes before this became an ugly argument. Jay's fuse was growing shorter by the day.

'Have you had lunch, béta?' Shubhra intervened.

Jay shook his head. 'I had snacks on the flight. I am not hungry.'

'I'll get tea.' Shubhra rushed to the kitchen.

Jay had already turned to face his father. 'Do you know how much I've struggled to get this deal, Dad? We have slogged our asses for this. We know we are the best. But still, I have to give a ten-crore bribe for this project.' Jay was speaking loudly now. 'But you won't understand this, Dad! With your holy and idealistic views!'

Satish refused to get provoked and continued quietly, 'Bribery never works. If your work is good, people will ask for you. You don't need to do dishonest things to make it, Jay.' Satish's words infuriated Jay further.

But Satish didn't seem to notice. Shubhra knew, now that Satish had started talking about this, he was not going to stop till he had said his piece. Jay took after him, and they were like two bulls, locking horns, always ready for a fight. She and Satish had raised Jay to be an independent thinker. Unfortunately, during the past couple of years, since he had started ALSOL, he had become extremely ambitious and arrogant. He seemed hell-bent on proving a point, especially to his dad.

Jay scoffed at his father and retorted, 'You don't have to tell me how to do business, Dad. I have made more money in two years than you made in your entire life!'

Satish's eyes narrowed as he gripped the sides of his chair. His knuckles began turning white. He had to remain calm. One of them had to. Or things would turn very ugly. He and Shubhra had talked about this, and he had promised her that he would not lose it. He clenched his jaw tightly and focused on keeping his breath steady.

Jay was still talking rapidly. 'Today's markets are very, *very* competitive. We don't have the luxury of time, Dad. You like playing small, because that keeps you safe from risks. All you have done is sit and push files. You, in fact, your *entire* generation, is filled with people who have never taken any risks. You are only interested in security and safety.'

Satish's voice trembled as he said softly, 'Security and safety has got us this house, béta. And you, your education. It also helped set up your business.'

Satish glanced towards the kitchen as he spoke. Shubhra was almost running towards them with a tray. She could see that her husband's face was darkening by the second.

Jay continued ranting without having heard his dad. 'One needs to dream big, and if I need to grease palms to get where I want to reach, I will do it. You are no one to tell me. It's none of your business! If one has to rise fast, one cannot have scruples.'

Satish opened his mouth to respond, but Shubhra banged the tray down between both the men in her beleaguered life. 'Stop it, both of you! Have your tea and samosas before they get cold.' She stood between father and son, handing them the teacups and snacks, and deliberately blocking their line of vision. Her ploy worked. It was infallible. It had kept the peace in their house for nearly three decades. 'You can continue fighting after you have eaten.' She knew that was not likely to happen.

Both ate in silence. Shubhra began talking of random stuff to ease the tension. 'How's Ritika?' she asked Jay. Ritika was Jay's girlfriend.

Jay seemed to lighten up at this. 'She's good. She wants to call you both over for dinner.'

Satish snorted, and Jay saw him scowl. 'What's your problem?' Jay snapped once more. Satish scoffed very softly and began picking on his samosa without looking up.

Shubhra quickly interjected, 'Shall I make gobhi parathas for you?' She knew Jay loved them.

But Jay had already got up. He shook his head. 'Next time, Ma. I need to sleep for a bit. Haven't slept all of last night.' Jay turned abruptly and ran up the stairs to his bedroom. Satish's eyes followed him; they were full of sadness.

Jay came down almost three hours later. He had changed into a T-shirt and cycling shorts. Satish was now sitting on the porch, reading the newspaper. He still looked visibly annoyed as he met Satish's gaze. Jay walked out the door without saying anything. It was dark outside. He went to the garage and wheeled out his sports bicycle. 'Bye, Ma,' he said as he snapped the bike helmet on.

Shubhra nodded silently. She suddenly looked very tired and resigned to her fate. Her eyes filled with tears as she watched Jay leave.

Satish continued reading the newspaper.

* * *

As Jay rode out on his bicycle, he called Raghav, his best friend. 'Hey Rags, are you free? I'll be at Ansal Plaza in ten minutes.'

Raghav was an engineer with a local construction company. He and Jay were school friends. Raghav was an amiable guy who was pretty happy with his life. He had married early and had a seven-year-old daughter, Arushi, who adored Jay.

Jay reached the parking lot a bit earlier than expected, but Raghav was already there. He was beaming and hugged Jay. 'Congratulations, Mr Tycoon!'

'For what? I haven't told you anything yet!' Jay grinned.

'Haha! What else can it be? You made a call to me suddenly today, after having gone underground for over one month! The tycoon must have been slogging away on something really big. Even his closest friend wasn't permitted to disturb him!'

'Okay, okay, Sherlock. Sorry for not taking your calls. But things were really tense. We sealed the deal a couple of hours ago. I'll have to pay them a hefty bribe. But we'll recover from it. The project is really big, Rags. It will bring ALSOL into the limelight. And, I want you with me on this.'

Raghav smiled. 'Big project means big responsibility. Less time for family and too much stress, Jay. You can handle it. I am not really cut out for that. I love my sleep too much!'

Jay shook his head. 'Yaar, you will never change! Even if god were to come and offer you an opportunity to make a fortune, you will refuse!'

Raghav nodded. 'It's all about priorities, Jay. I am really lucky to have a wife like Reema. We are really happy with what we have. She made me realize this as soon as we met each other, as you know. Every day I get home by 7 p.m., and the three of us eat together. They're always waiting for me. Then, we chit-chat, watch some TV and go to sleep. It's a good life, Jay, but not your cup of tea!'

'I really envy you, Rags. *Mujhse to kabhi nahi hoga*. I won't be able to do it, ever. I cannot sit idle for a moment. I feel life will pass me by, and I will be old before I know it, having achieved nothing.'

Raghav laughed. 'You are you and I am me, Jay. I cannot be you and you can't be me. We cannot be anyone else but ourselves. Isn't it? That's what makes us all so different. Problems arise when we want to be someone we're not.'

Jay loved Raghav for these insights. He was a simple soul and never forced himself on anybody. And Jay ran to him whenever he needed to calm down. Raghav never questioned Jay. He had always been happy for Jay ever since they became friends at school. It was Raghav who helped Jay claw back after every failed relationship. He was the only one who had stood by Jay whenever he had clashed with his father and walked out of his house, helping them patch up. Jay depended on him. Whenever Jay needed him, Raghav was always there.

'What happened? Fight with uncle again?' Raghav had learnt to read the signs.

Jay's words came out in a torrent. 'He just doesn't feel happy with any of my successes, Rags. He says I am going too fast. Young man in a hurry. He wants me to play safe and not give money under the table to get projects. You tell me, Rags, in this day and age, how can I get ahead that way? If I don't grease palms, someone else will. I can't risk losing a good project just because of morals, yaar.'

Raghav was a good listener. Jay's outburst ended, and Raghav kept quiet for a few moments. 'Maybe he has a point, Jay. He is from the previous generation and looks at life very differently. Everyone has a point of view. You. Me. Your dad. Even my little Arushi. But, why does his disapproval bother you so much, Jay?'

'He's my dad, dammit.' Jay's phone buzzed in the pocket of his shorts. It was a message from Ritika: *Where are you?*

Raghav nodded and didn't say anything. Jay typed quickly: *Sorry Ritz. Busy day.* He kept talking as he scrolled through his messages. 'Rags, I need him to understand that I'm not some two-bit criminal. I am doing this for him. And for Ma.'

'When we let things be, they let us be, Jay. I believe that things always turn out for the best. *Just let things be,*' Raghav said softly.

Jay looked up in surprise. This was the second time he'd heard those words. In the morning, it was Ashwini Kumar Singh who had said something similar, and now Rags. Jay was silent.

Raghav saw that Jay was listening to him intently. 'Jay, I am really happy to know of your deal, but please be careful. Pay the bribe after everything is signed, and after they pay the advance.'

'Yes, absolutely.' Jay was typing away on his phone: *Reaching in 20.*

'Why don't you join us next Wednesday? Asiad Village. It's our monthly meeting. Thursday is a holiday, so we will all be relaxed. Chintan is in town, so everyone is going to be there.' Raghav was referring to the monthly meeting of their classmates.

Jay's phone buzzed again: *Let's go to Frisky Mamba. Timmy and Puja will be there too :).*

Jay scowled. He hated them. 'Nah! Too caught up, yaar,' Jay said to Raghav, trying to wriggle out.

But Raghav caught on. 'I know that nowadays you don't decide these things.' Raghav lightly tapped on Jay's arm, gripping his phone. 'She does.' Jay frowned and jerked his arm back instantly. Raghav shook his head, 'Jay, you are totally under her influence.'

'Rags, please don't start this all over again,' Jay hissed. 'I should leave now.'

Raghav was quick to retract. 'Yes, I have to get home too. Arushi's math homework. Reema asked me to come early.'

Jay nodded as he mounted his cycle.

'Congrats once again,' Raghav continued. 'Hope to see you next Wednesday at Asiad.'

'Don't,' Jay replied curtly. 'I will see if I can make it, but please don't expect me.'

Raghav looked on, shaking his head, as Jay quickly pedalled out of the parking lot, without looking back.

5

Curse of the Dead Man

Word had got around that Vini was sharing a very interesting tale. When Vini came down from his room, he remembered to carry his ektara. Vini noticed two young men waiting at the bottom of the stairs. One of them was from the locality, and Vini had seen him at the majlis the previous evening. The man was a software engineer with an MNC. He saluted Vini.

'Namaste, Viniji. My name is Suketu,' the man said. He wanted to know if his friend could join the majlis and hear Vini speak.

'Of course. All are welcome,' Vini said. As they began walking towards the gathering, Vini noticed a small group of men and women following them. They were all simply dressed. Suketu said, 'They are my friends, Viniji. We all work at different offices and volunteer for *seva* activities. We send food packets to flood-affected areas; we collect old clothes, newspapers, etc. We don't have any formal organization. Everyone is welcome. We have seen your videos on YouTube. I came to know that you were speaking here and shared it in our social media group. We all are keen to hear you speak and guide our group. I do hope you don't mind, sir.'

Vini nodded silently. It was heartening to see that the youth were keen to do good work. In a world filled with turmoil, people were lost and needed direction. Vini noticed that someone had put, on a slightly raised platform, a cushion for him to sit on, and had also placed a microphone and a bottle of water. Quite a few people were sitting all around, on durries and on chairs. It was a relaxed and happy atmosphere. Vini guessed that they must have shared with each other what he'd told them on the previous days. When he arrived, many of them stood up. Vini bowed to them with folded hands and quietly sat in their midst. 'You don't need to stand up. Let's keep it informal. Thank you for coming. I am sure our evenings together will be fruitful and enjoyable.'

'Tell us about success. Why do successful people often become hurtful and nasty?' asked Suketu.

'Aah! The heady feeling of success! When you seem to be doing everything right, life is smooth-sailing, and everything just falls into place. You feel so powerful! That's exactly what had happened to Ash. Success had gone to his head.

'Success is a heady drug. You are walking on clouds and the world is at your feet. You want more and more of this heady feeling. The moment you have achieved something big, you want to dwarf it with a greater feat, a grander accomplishment.

'Nothing appears to have the power to stop you. And yet, it will happen. Not today, not tomorrow, but someday, the dream run will end, and, if you had been brash when you rode the crest of the wave of success, the end won't be very pleasant. You'll fall hard and alone. And if you had been flying too high, soaring on the winds of fortune, then the fall might be pretty painful too,' Vini said, sighing softly.

He closed his eyes and sang,

'Charde sooraj dhalde wekhe,
bujhde deewe balde wekhe,
Heere da koi mul na jaane,
khote sikke chalde wekhe,
Jinna'n da na jag te koi,
o vi puttar palde wekhe,
Aohdi rehmat de naal bande,
pani utte chalde wekhe,
Loki kehnde daal ni galdi,
mein te pathar galde wekhe,
Jinha qadar na kitti rabb di,
hatth khali o malde wekhe'

As was Vini's inimitable style, he then translated the beautiful words of Bulleh Shah,

'Rising suns I have seen setting,
dying lamps I have seen flare up,
No one knows the real value of a diamond,
fake coins I have seen honoured,
Ones with nobody in this world,
I have seen such orphans nurtured,
Bestowed with divine grace,

I have seen men walk on water,
People say they never succeed,
I have seen rocks melt for the determined,
Those with no respect for god,
I have seen wringing empty hands.'

After a few moments of silence, Vini began the tale of Ash once again.

* * *

Ash sat holding the crumpled letter for a long time. He wanted to destroy the confounded piece of paper immediately, but he just couldn't do it. A voice screamed inside his head, 'Burn the damn thing, Ash!' But simultaneously, another calmer voice said, 'Today was your wake-up call, Ash. Keep this letter with you. Read it every day.'

Ash noticed that dawn was breaking. He stood up coming to a decision. He folded the letter slowly and put it away inside his safe along with other papers and valuables. Then, he changed into running clothes and walked out of his house. He looked at his Rolex: it was nearly 6 a.m. He tried to run, but his body felt stiff from the night's vagaries and his lack of sleep. He needed to clear his mind, so he decided on a brisk walk. A few morning-walkers passed by him occasionally. Some people recognized him and greeted him. One acquaintance buttonholed him for a couple of minutes before he could make good his escape. Ash was in no mood for small talk and decided that it would be best to get off the beaten path. He turned towards a disused footpath so that he could be alone, with his own thoughts.

He walked quickly down an incline into a wooded area. Trees and shrubs were growing untended, and he had to manoeuvre around them. After a few minutes he had lost his sense of direction. He kept walking and, as the sun peeked over the horizon, arrived at a large rock half-buried on a raised mound. He had never before noticed the rock or the mound it stood upon. But then, he never really noticed anything if it wasn't useful or profitable to him.

Ash saw cans and bottles strewn around and guessed that young people came there to party. The large rock had a flat vertical face, with tender grass growing at its bottom. The place looked inviting, and Ash decided to sit down for a bit and watch the day breaking. He leaned against the rock and stretched his legs in front of him. Light fell on his face as the sun came up slowly. The tiredness of the sleepless night overtook him, and his eyes began to droop. He fell asleep with the sun shining on his face.

Ash was standing on a vast, empty plain. There was nothing around him. He looked up at the sky and saw a bright point of light. As he watched, the point began to expand, and he realized that it was gradually taking on a humanoid form, silvery bluish in colour. Gradually, the apparition took on the form of a man as Ash continued to stare, fascinated.

The man was floating far, far away, bathed in white light. He had his arms outstretched and was falling backwards. Behind him was vast, black, empty space. Ash wanted to reach out and stop him. He wanted to ask him something very important, but he didn't know what.

Ash leaped high into the sky. He was weightless. He flew towards the rapidly falling man. As he neared the man, he realized that the apparition was much larger than his own form. The apparition's face was inscrutable and kept changing. Some faces that formed were familiar, while others were unknown.

Ash was floating over the kaleidoscopic spectre. He wanted to stop the apparition from falling. He dived towards the apparition and gradually came face to face with the formless entity. He reached out to grasp at the incorporeal form. It was then that he realized that he, too, was incorporeal.

Ash's inertia caused him to continue his dive, and he began flailing his arms as he made contact with the apparition. There was a flash of white light, and Ash began to sink into the incorporeal form. He tried to scream, but he had no voice. The apparition morphed into the man who had died in front of him the previous night.

Ash was no more Ash. He was being annihilated completely by the dead man. The apparition had almost consumed him entirely. In the final moments, as Ash dissolved into the form, the apparition began to laugh as it transformed into Ash, swallowing him completely . . .

* * *

Vini stopped. The silence was deafening. He took a sip of water. Some birds squawked at a distance. Vini didn't want the magic to break and continued softly, 'Ash woke up with a start . . .'

* * *

The sun was high up. Ash looked at his watch: 9.25 a.m. He had slept for over three hours, leaning against the rock. He leaped up, trying to orient himself. He saw a plume of smoke rising into the sky from where he stood. The walking track could be seen clearly, beyond the undergrowth, hardly 300 metres from him. Ash hurried down the mound. Dusting himself, he turned to go back to his house as a few people eyed him curiously.

When he reached home, he immediately sensed that something wasn't right. He found the front door open and entered the house. As he walked through the corridor, he could hear landline phones ringing incessantly over the blaring sounds of the television. 'What's going on?' he wondered as he walked into the living room. Pratima was sitting on the edge of the divan, her eyes glued to the television. A few servants were standing on the sides and watching. Everyone had anxious expressions on their faces. Ash frowned and turned to look at the television screen. 'Mangal, get me some water,' he barked at his oldest servant, who rushed off instantly.

The newsreader was talking excitedly. Ash heard his name being uttered. Someone had anonymously sent a

CD to all major news channels and newspaper offices detailing every illegal deal done by Ash, along with meticulously collected proof. There were unconfirmed reports of large deposits in international tax havens and of huge amounts of cash and gold that Ash had supposedly hidden away. The channels claimed to have all the details.

Before Ash could react he heard the wailing of sirens. Ash's heart began thumping in panic. He stood in a state of shock. Beads of cold sweat began forming on his forehead. He was certain that this was the doing of the man who had committed suicide the previous evening at the party. He didn't know what to do.

* * *

Vini looked at the people listening to him and said, 'Life has strange ways to bring us back to the ground when we are flying too high. One should never forget that there's a much higher power that balances our actions. It takes just a single gust of wind to make a carefully constructed house of cards collapse. That's what Ash's entire life was, a fragile house of cards.' Vini sighed and continued the story.

* * *

The next few days were a complete blur. Ash's house and offices were sealed. Tax raids began simultaneously in seven locations. The Anti-Corruption Bureau went hammer and tongs after all his dealings. Ash was detained in judicial custody for questioning. He was grilled by the Enforcement Directorate, the Anti-Corruption Bureau, the Income Tax Department and many other agencies for over eighteen hours a day. None of his politician friends came to his aid. Ash's office staff had no sympathy for him, and each and every person testified against him.

Ash went into complete shock. He began calling his downfall 'Curse of the Dead Man'. He had no clue as to who had given out the details of all his dubious deals to the dead man. Things began spiralling downwards rapidly. As Ash's lawyers tried every trick in the book, as well as every ploy outside of law, to save him from imprisonment, he received another setback. A scrupulously honest municipal commissioner, who had recently taken charge, demolished an entire row of shops owned by Ash, deeming them illegal, and levied hefty fines. This was the last straw that broke the camel's back.

Ash flew into a terrible rage. He didn't listen to anyone and called an impromptu press conference the moment he was released from judicial custody. He pointed fingers at a powerful minister, insinuating that the minister had been taking hefty bribes on behalf of the chief minister, and that Ash was being made a scapegoat. The strategy boomeranged, and Ash found that a thorough and vengeful scrutiny of all his assets began on a war footing.

The police swooped down on his house in the middle of the night. It was the oldest trick in the book. Ash was arrested for possession of drugs that the police had planted themselves. He was put behind bars without bail by order of an extremely vindictive chief minister. Soon, other cases, some real and some fabricated, were brought against him. All his assets were frozen. Three non-bailable warrants were issued against him from as many different states, including a case of attempted rape by a woman whom Ash had met briefly at a party, years ago.

* * *

Vini stopped again. He had a faraway look on his face. Speaking about that time wasn't easy for him. But he realized that this was his real test.

When one talks about an unpleasant past without getting perturbed, one is truly free of its burden. Vini smiled wryly to himself before continuing impassively.

* * *

Ash remained locked up for over six months. Gradually, all his assets were sold off. In prison, he was mocked, jeered and even hit by the inmates. Without any money, he couldn't continue with his lawyers, who also jumped ship quickly. The state provided him with an inexperienced lawyer with limited knowledge of his cases. Ash had begun to withdraw into a shell.

Immediately after all this happened, his wife Pratima filed for a divorce, and he decided not to contest it. He didn't want to see her when she came to say goodbye. Some days later, he came to know that the dead man had been a childhood friend of Pratima's father. She had adored this man when she was a kid. Ash was quite certain that it was she who had given out all the details to the dead man. But somehow, he didn't really care any more. Pratima left the country, taking the girls with her.

Ash was shifted to the regular prison with petty criminals, where he refused to pay his respects to a small-time gangster. Within a day, he got into a fracas with the goon's minions, after he had refused to wash their dirty plates and spoons, and was thrashed by them. Ash retaliated and punched one of them in the face, drawing blood. The furious goon instantly pulled out a knife and stabbed Ash in the stomach. He was left for dead, bleeding on the floor of the mess area.

The news reached the authorities, who took their time in shifting Ash to the prison hospital. They waited until the ministry was informed. A go-ahead was given after taking sufficient time to ensure Ash wouldn't survive. For three long hours, Ash drifted between life and death.

* * *

Vini spoke almost in a whisper. 'When we hover at the edge, on the boundary between life and death, nothing matters at all, my dear friends. Nothing, except four questions,

What am I?
Why am I here?

What do I want from my life?
What's the point of everything?'

The majlis sat dumbstruck. Vini let the silence, pregnant with the powerful questions, permeate into the listeners before he continued.

* * *

Ash's mind had gone blank. He couldn't see any meaning in whatever he had made the mainstay of his entire existence. Money, fame and power, nothing made sense to him any more as he felt his life ebbing away. His entire life flashed in front of his eyes. His parents, siblings, Pratima and his daughters—they all looked sad and hurt. There weren't any pleasant memories. He could only see himself fighting and people walking away from him. He didn't feel any attachment with anyone at all. He hadn't ever cared for any of them. One thing that kept coming back to him again and again was the dying man and his prophetic words.

He was floating through a long tunnel
  with no end in sight.
  There was no pain or pleasure.
  He didn't feel anything at all . . .
  Only a sense of falling,
  tumbling through nothingness.
  Then, he saw his mother's face,
  full of love and tears.

She was holding him in her arms.
He had just been born.
She held him to her bosom and laughed.
He felt her warmth and her comfortable smell.
She cooed lovingly into his ears,
'Aaashuuu . . .'
He laughed and then grimaced.
He felt a sharp stab in his stomach.

'We got a pulse. He's back.' Ash could hear an anxious voice, far away.

'Aaashuuu . . . my son. I love you.
You have a long life ahead, béta . . .
Go and embrace the world, my son . . .'

'Ashwini . . . Ash? Can you hear me? Give me a sign, Ash!'
    Ash grimaced as he tried to laugh once again. His mother's face was fading away, but he knew she would be there, waiting for him, when the time came for him to depart. But now wasn't the time. 'Aaah!' he groaned. Ash was a fighter, and the doctors in the jail were sincere. They saved his life.
    The government, to save itself any further embarrassment, wound up the vendetta against him and ordered his release. By the time Ash was allowed to leave the prison hospital, a month later, he virtually had nothing and nowhere to go.

* * *

Vini ended the majlis on a pensive note, with Shankaracharya's verse,

'Punarapi jananam punarapi maranam
punarapi jananee jathare shayanam,
Iha samsare bahudustaare
kripayaa paare paahi murare.'

'Taking birth and dying repeatedly, sleeping in a mother's womb again and again,
This illusory world is tough to cross. O Lord, help me transcend, with your grace.'

6

Mindless Love

Jay reached Ritika's flat in Hauz Khas in ten minutes. Actually, he was the one paying the rent on the swanky duplex apartment. They were, more or less, living together. Jay used his own keys to enter. Ritika was in their bedroom upstairs. Jay called out from the lower floor.

'Hey, Ritz! I got the amusement park deal! Let's celebrate. I'll call for some . . .'

Ritika breezed out of the bedroom and stood on the landing. She looked ravishing. All five feet eleven inches of her in her six-inch stilettos. She was dressed to the hilt in an expensive black dress that was split down one side. Her face was fully made up, and her copper-streaked hair fell in a tumble across her cheeks, accentuating the large solitaires that adorned her ears.

'Wow, Ritz! You're looking stunning!' Jay exclaimed as he raised an eyebrow, impressed.

But Ritika was frowning. 'Super news. But what took you so long, Jay? she demanded in her high-pitched nasal voice. 'Timmy's done the booking for

9 p.m. And it takes hours to get to Gurgaon! Can you please hurry up?'

'Why did Timmy book the place?' Jay still stood at the bottom of the stairs, gripping the banister with one hand. He had to look up to talk to her.

'I messaged you.'

Jay knew there was trouble brewing. He didn't wish to get into an argument. He needed peace and quiet after the hectic day. He quickly ran up the stairs and tried to kiss her. Ritika moved her head away to one side, scowling. He immediately began to placate her. 'Sure, darling. I saw your message. But I don't want to go there. I want to chill at home. Just you and me.' He nuzzled her hair. 'Umm. You smell so good.'

Ritika snorted and jerked away. Jay knew when he was beaten.

He decided to play along. 'I was just teasing you, Ritzy.' She yielded a bit. Jay whispered, 'Of course we'll go. Anyway, what's the occasion?'

'You've forgotten, as usual. It's their anniversary. You never remember anything, Jay.'

'Oh! Okay then. Let me get changed. I'll take a quick shower. Let's leave in ten minutes.' Jay rushed off before Ritika could bring up something else. It was never just one thing. She had this uncanny habit of connecting completely unrelated stuff from the past to checkmate him. God only knew how she remembered such things—like when he had worn which shirt or where they had eaten a certain dish or who had said what to whom, at which party. Everything seemed to be filed away in that small head of hers in full HD, ready to be accessed at any moment. Handling women was just not his thing. Give him ten Hoodas to deal with any day.

Ritika was an aspiring model whom Jay had met at a friend's party around eighteen months ago. He had fallen head over heels for her, and within two weeks they were dating. He was besotted. She didn't have a place to stay, and less than a month after their first meeting, Jay rented a fully furnished place for her, and for himself, much to his parents' chagrin. With Ritika's arrival, a lot had changed in Jay's life. Now, he was constantly fighting with his dad and his friends, and he refused to hear a single word against her.

Ritika was on a call when he came out. 'Just leaving now, Poo. Love you.' Ritika puckered her lips and let out a loud smack into the phone's mic.

Within minutes of leaving Hauz Khas, they were caught in a traffic snarl. As much as he loved driving his two-seater Mercedes-Benz whenever he got the chance, Jay wasn't enjoying this drive at all. He detested gridlocks. Anyway, he had simply wanted to chill at home. He wasn't really excited to meet up with Ritika's freeloading friends. And to top all of this, Ritika was constantly nagging him throughout the ride.

'Why do you do this to me, Jay? You left before I was up and didn't even tell me that you were flying to Mumbai! And, you haven't been taking my calls all day.'

Jay retorted softly, 'I have been terribly busy in meetings all day, Ritz. It is a really big contract. Very important clients.' He just wanted to turn and head back home. Why was he doing this to himself? Some unnamed fear stopped him from blowing up at Ritz the way he would on his dad and on Raghav. He felt that he was walking on eggshells with her.

'I don't care about your bloody clients. All you do is work, work, work! You don't give me any time at all!'

Jay cursed and banged his fist on the steering wheel, swerving the car and almost hitting the central divider.

Ritika screamed. 'What's wrong with you, Jay? Do you want to kill me?' She started to sob.

'Sorry, babe!' Jay immediately apologized. His body was tingling with the adrenaline rush after the swerve. They both kept quiet for the rest of the journey. Once they crossed into Gurgaon, the road was relatively empty, and they finally reached Frisky Mamba at 9.30 p.m.

Timmy and Puja were halfway through their drinks and snacks. Ritika instantly cheered up on meeting them. Puja had ordered for Ritika, but not for Jay. This was a regular feature. Ritika would totally forget Jay the moment she met the couple. They were friends from college days. All three more or less ignored Jay, and kept chatting and cracking jokes among themselves, until the bill arrived. Today was no different. Jay wasn't in a mood to talk anyway. And he was driving, so he didn't want to drink. He called for fresh orange juice. The music was loud and drowned any opportunity of inane conversation, which he found convenient. He began scrolling through his emails.

By 10.30 p.m., Ritika was already quite drunk. Timmy had been plying her with tequilas constantly.

Jay wasn't too happy to see this. He tried to stop her, but she sneered at him and downed three more tequila shots in quick succession. Jay got annoyed and told her to control herself. But Ritika was in no mood to stop. Timmy intervened, asking Jay to let her be. Jay turned and snapped at him, telling him to stay out of this.

Ritika now began to make a scene, just to spite Jay. She took a knife and fork and started banging on the table, singing along to the music. Jay looked alarmed and tried to stop her, but Ritika started mouthing expletives with the music. She clambered on her chair, swaying to the music. As Puja and Timmy tried to calm her down she picked up a plate and a glass, and began banging them together, until they slipped and shattered on the floor.

A few waiters rushed in. Someone ran to call the manager. Everything was happening too fast. Ritika began teetering as the chair began to tip over. Jay leaped to grab her. Ritika struggled out of his grip and fell on the floor. She kicked at a waiter who tried to help her up and began to hurl abuses on the men sweeping the broken china. Then she began demanding more drinks from the barman, abusing him when he refused, before passing out.

The manager was livid. He came up to Timmy and said that he was calling the cops. Puja looked ready to cry. Three female staff—a receptionist and two waitresses—were trying to prop Ritika on a chair. Timmy looked pleadingly at Jay, who guessed immediately that the bum had no money on him.

Jay finally intervened. 'I am really so sorry. What's the damage?'

The manager turned to him, realizing that he had been addressing the wrong person. 'Sir, this is really not good. Your bill is around eight thousand or so. I haven't had it calculated so far. But there is a lot of damage and breakage. And our other clients have been disturbed. At least twenty-five thousand, sir. We don't expect this kind of behaviour from our respected clients.'

'Really sorry about this. I'll tell you what I can do. Over and above the bill, I will give you five thousand to cover your breakages and another two for tips. Total fifteen thousand. That should be enough. Now, can you please ask your staff to help the lady to my car immediately?' Before the manager could say anything, Jay fished out his credit card.

Within minutes he had Ritika seated in the car. He ignored Timmy and Puja completely. 'Bloody leeches!' he growled as he drove off.

She was mumbling curses throughout the ride back to their apartment. The road was quite clear, and they made it back in under forty minutes.

Jay pulled her out of the car, and lugged her into the apartment and all the way upstairs, into their bedroom. 'Don't touch me, you bastard! Where's Puja? I want to party . . . Who are you to bring me back? You bastard . . .' She was constantly abusing him in her befuddled state.

'We'll talk tomorrow,' Jay said softly. He pursed his lips and sighed as he tucked her in bed. He lay down next to her gingerly, without changing his clothes. Despite Ritika's tantrums, he found her very vulnerable. That's what had attracted him to her. She needed him. He found her so fragile, like a porcelain doll. He had to protect her. He had to save her from the big bad world. He blamed her lowlife friends for the mess she had become. He had to stop her from meeting those lowlifes.

It was nearly midnight. In the semi-darkness, Jay stared at the ceiling and the whirring fan, wondering about his long day. He turned and watched Ritika sleeping. Her breathing was uneven. Mascara had stained her face and the satin pillowcase. She was scowling even in her sleep.

'What am I doing?' Jay thought to himself. He turned and lay on his back once more, staring at the spinning fan. Glimpses of the entire day flashed before his eyes. Encountering Ashwini Kumar Singh at the lounge, the business deal in Mumbai, Hooda and his cronies, negotiating the bribe, the fight with his dad, meeting Raghav and Ritika's scene at Frisky Mamba . . . What a day it had been!

Out of all the things, his early-morning encounter with Vini and the conversation at the airport lounge kept coming back to him again and again.

* * *

'Jay! I have nothing to wear for Saturday's party! I need that Vero Moda dress! The shop guy called to say that it's come. Let's go to Ambience Mall today, please!' Ritika was on her sweetest behaviour when she wanted something. Jay knew that there was no use arguing with her. She always got her way with him.

'Sure, Ritz. But I can only be back home after five. Back-to-back meetings. Have you seen my red polo?' Jay muttered distractedly as he searched for his favourite T-shirt. He wasn't interested in high fashion and liked comfort clothing.

'Jay, why can't you get something better to wear?'

Jay just shook his head without looking at her. 'Not now, Ritz. I am in a rush. We'll talk about this in the evening.' Hurriedly, he yanked out a yellow polo T-shirt and pulled it over his head as he ran out with his briefcase and mobile. Ritika rolled her eyes.

It had been ten days since Jay had paid Hooda the bribe. Jay had organized Rs 10 crore with great difficulty, since Shyam had been holidaying in Paris. Somehow, everything had been managed, and Jay had delivered the cash to Sagar on time. They had got the letter of intent and were waiting for the final papers to be signed by Sharma.

Shyam had returned a week after the deal was finalized, and all the partners had celebrated along with their families the previous evening. Jay's father had refused to join, and his mother had tactfully declared that she wasn't feeling too well. This had led to another heated exchange, and a row had nearly erupted.

Jay came home at 4.30 p.m., a bit earlier than expected. He wanted to crash for a while, but Ritika insisted on going shopping immediately. He was irritable as they left for the mall but said nothing.

Nowadays, he had started thinking twice before coming home early. Ritika never asked him if he was okay. The magic seemed to be going out of their relationship.

'If you don't like to drive, you should keep a driver,' she said.

'I love driving, darling. But not to a mall. And, you know very well that I don't like anyone else driving my Merc. You should have gone in a cab,' Jay said coldly.

'Actually, you don't like driving me around. Why don't you just say so?'

Jay didn't reply. She was right, but there was no point in starting her off again. Ritika kept goading him in a sneering tone. 'You don't want to spend your precious money on another car. You don't care about me at all.'

Jay was scowling. It was *always* about her. Why the hell did he put up with her nonsense? He gripped the steering wheel tightly and his knuckles started going white. 'It's not about another car, Ritz. You simply want me to drive you around. I do have a lot of work, you know.'

'Hmph!' Ritika grunted. 'I don't have a choice, Jay.' Then, she pulled out the ace in her arsenal. 'If you have such a problem with me, why don't you dump me, like all your other girlfriends?' She knew what his reaction would be.

'Darling, I didn't mean it that way at all. I am sorry. Please don't be upset.'

Checkmate. Ritika smirked inwardly. She had Jay cornered. He wasn't her first catch. She was adept at reading the signs. She and Jay had, maybe, another couple of months, at the most. Timmy and Puja had introduced her to Sahil Mahtani, a flamboyant restaurateur, just the previous week, a few days after the Frisky Mamba fiasco. He seemed to be a good catch. She had to act fast. Jay seemed to be on to her game. She couldn't milk him for too long now.

'Here we are.' Jay stopped at the mall entrance and gave the car keys to the valet. Ritika chuckled sarcastically. 'What now?' Jay asked.

'Valets are allowed to touch your precious Merc, I guess.'

Jay grinned. 'That's necessary. Can't be helped, darling,' he said as they walked through the security scanner.

Things started going downhill once more, the moment they finished with Ritika's purchases. She had already put Jay on the back foot in the car, and he kept quiet as she went crazy on her shopping binge. Suddenly, she remembered their morning argument about Jay's T-shirt, and pulled an unwilling Jay towards the men's clothing section. Jay didn't want to buy anything at all, but finally chose a couple of simple shirts and T-shirts to keep the peace. He would habitually look at the price tags before deciding.

Ritika saw this and became caustic. 'Still pinching pennies, I see!' Jay bit his lip. He simply switched off as she forced him to purchase several other shirts that he didn't really want.

Back in the car, Jay was fuming in silence as he drove back. Ritika began mocking him and his parents for their 'small-town mentality' when it came to spending on expensive stuff despite having loads of money. 'Look, Ritz, it's none of your business. Have I stopped you from buying whatever you want? Do I comment on you or your family? You don't need to pull my parents into this, Ritz. Don't provoke me. I can also say a lot, but I don't.'

'Jay, stop shouting at me . . .'

'YOU STOP YOUR BLOODY NONSENSE FIRST, RITZ!' Jay shouted.

Ritika began sobbing. Jay was breathing hard. He braked suddenly at a red signal, and Ritika lurched ahead. Had it not been for the seatbelt, she would have hit her head on the windshield. The packages of clothes they'd bought tumbled and fell on the floor of the Merc.

'WATCH IT, JAY! You are going to kill us!' Ritika was crying now.

Jay came to his senses. What was he doing? They could have died. 'Sorry, Ritz. Didn't mean to do that. Sorry, sorry, sorry . . .' Jay tried to calm his breathing as he watched the countdown on the traffic-signal timer: 110 . . . 109 . . . 108 . . . 107 . . .

'I want to meet Puja and Timmy.' Ritika sniffled.

That was not going to happen. Jay had had enough. He had no intention of meeting those leeches. His phone beeped just as the signal turned green. Raghav.

Jay suddenly remembered Raghav telling him about the meet-up at Asiad. He must have sent a reminder, Jay guessed as he drove towards Hauz Khas. Looking straight ahead, Jay said, 'Sorry, Ritz, not today.' His tone was jubilant. 'I am meeting up with my schoolmates tonight. I committed last week. Sorry I didn't tell you. Must have slipped my mind. You can go alone and meet them if you like. I'll call you a cab.'

Ritika looked at him strangely. Jay thought she was in shock, but she wasn't. She was actually surprised at herself. She had miscalculated. Her time with Jay was over already. Good that he was going off on his own. She now had time to plan.

As soon as she got back into the apartment, Ritika called Puja. 'Heyyy, Poo! Can we meet up for dinner? Only me. Jay's busy. He won't be joining us. In fact, I was wondering if we could meet up with Sahil tonight. He's too cute.'

Jay decided to take some time to cool off and drove around aimlessly. He wanted to sit with Raghav and talk, letting it all out. Raghav was such a good listener. He always helped Jay clear his mind before he took any major decisions. But Raghav was going to be at Asiad. Maybe he could go there and pull him out of the party after a bit, and they could sit somewhere and chat. Or maybe he would enjoy the party. Meeting his classmates was not such a bad idea, after all. He could play it by the ear.

He called Raghav. 'Hey, Rags. What time are you reaching Asiad? I'll meet you there. Ya . . . ya! I am coming. Haha. Yes, you could say that. Ritika made me decide that I should meet up with you all.'

The wind was blowing through his hair. He suddenly felt much lighter after calling Raghav. He switched the car stereo on. His favourite song, 'Something Just like This', was always on loop. He hummed along with

Chris Martin as he turned his car on to an empty forest road near Vasant Kunj.

These solitary drives calmed him. Somehow, his Merc seemed to come alive and responded to his lightest touch when he was alone. He smiled to himself. He secretly thought of his car as a woman, the way seafaring captains talk of their ships. She understood him and seemed to share his thoughts, and he felt that she became an extension of him during these quiet moments.

He drove around for twenty minutes before turning to go and meet with his classmates.

7

The Beedi Shop

The next evening, when Vini reached the majlis he noticed that the number of listeners had nearly doubled from the previous evening. Some people wished to ask him about their own problems, and Vini patiently answered them before continuing with Ash's story.

'Please talk to us about anger,' a young man asked.

'We get angry with people whose actions directly affect us. We do not become angry about things that don't concern us. You won't care if a cook in another city burned some unknown person's lunch. But you could get angry at your cook if it was your lunch that was burnt. Sometimes we get upset when things don't go our way, or we are prevented from doing what we want to. The wise ones realize that everyone is an empty boat,' Vini replied.

The listeners exchanged baffled glances.

'Well, let me tell you all a story. A man bought a new boat and decided to go fishing in a lake. After a while, he dozed off in the warm afternoon. Suddenly, he felt a hard bump as another boat collided with his boat.

He was angry that his new boat had been damaged by some stupid person and cursed loudly as he opened his eyes. But when he turned, he saw that it was an empty boat which had probably come untethered and floated out. Who could the man shout at now?

'Our anger is inside us. People are like empty boats that bump into us, and we become upset. As soon as we recognize that we are in control of how we react to whatever happens to us, we will stop getting angry. This is exactly what happened to Ash. When he was released from jail, he found that all his assets were gone. No one came to meet him. Everything that he had built his entire existence around, suddenly felt meaningless . . .'

Ash didn't feel anything at all. No sadness or anger. Nothing.

* * *

Ash's near-death experience had changed him completely. He had no interest in looking back. He went back to his house, which had been sold. It was just wood, glass, metal, plastic, bricks and stones. He didn't have any sentimental attachment to it. All his personal possessions were packed and stored in a room, and his old servant, Mangal, was the only one who had stayed back, awaiting his return.

Mangal had taken care of Ash since he was a boy. He cried when he saw Ash's condition. Ash asked him to take whatever he wanted and dispose of the rest of his possessions. Mangal refused to leave and tended to Ash for a month at the guest house he was putting up in, until the stab wound healed completely. Then, he too left for his village. Mangal wanted Ash to come with him. Ash thanked him and took his address. But right now, he wanted some time to himself. He had so many questions that needed answers. The words of Henley's 'Invictus' played in his head over and over:

> Out of the night that covers me,
> Black as the pit from pole to pole,
> I thank whatever gods may be
> For my unconquerable soul.
>
> In the fell clutch of circumstance
> I have not winced nor cried aloud.
> Under the bludgeonings of chance
> My head is bloody, but unbowed.
>
> Beyond this place of wrath and tears
> Looms but the Horror of the shade,
> And yet the menace of the years
> Finds and shall find me unafraid.
>
> It matters not how strait the gate,
> How charged with punishments the scroll,
> I am the master of my fate,
> I am the captain of my soul.

Ash closed down all his bank accounts, met his lawyers and asked them to wind up whatever little was left

of his assets, take their fee and send the rest to his
daughters. Once everything was done, he left the city.

Ash wandered aimlessly for almost a year. He
travelled in buses and trains. He went on long treks,
met many interesting people, but peace eluded him.
He listened to the discourses of many wise men,
teachers and healers. He went and stayed at places
that people called holy and blessed, he tried different
meditation techniques, he tried fasting and lived on
one meal a day for months, but he couldn't feel any
joy or peace. Eventually, he decided to go and visit
Mangal at his village.

Mangal now ran a pan-and-beedi shop in his
village. His older children had left the village looking
for better opportunities, and Mangal lived with his wife
and youngest son, who was still in high school. Mangal
was really happy to see Ash. But Ash said he would
stay with Mangal and his family on one condition—he
wanted to work and pay for his stay. Mangal refused
outright, but Ash didn't budge. Finally, Mangal agreed,
and Ash began to run the shop for him.

Ash was really grateful to Mangal. His interest
in the material world was gradually being rekindled.
He saw the shop as a good business opportunity, and
his sharp business mind began working overtime. He
suggested that they make a few changes in order to
make Mangal's business grow more efficiently. With a
small investment, they could make a lot more money.
Mangal refused politely, saying he was satisfied with
what came his way. A bigger business meant more
responsibilities and unnecessary worries. Mangal and

his family were happy with their small income. They lived well within their means, and thus they had a stress-free life, with a lot of time for themselves. Ash shook his head in disbelief.

A few days after his arrival at the village, Ash encountered an old man who came to the shop for a packet of beedis. He wore an old, white, half-sleeve cotton vest over a white pyjama and worn-out bathroom slippers on his calloused feet, his heels were cracked and blackened. He carried an ektara in one hand. Ash saw many people touch his feet. The pot-bellied man was stocky, and had a grey stubble and cropped grey hair. His greyish eyes watered, saliva leaked from the edges of his mouth and he had blackened teeth, half of which were missing. Ash gave him a packet of beedis and asked for the money. As the old man fumbled trying to take money out from a hidden pocket inside his vest, Mangal reverentially stopped him with folded hands. He bowed to the old man, who raised his hand in a gesture of blessing as he left with the beedis.

Every few days the man would turn up, and Ash's benefactor gave him beedis without taking any money from him. Mangal had categorically instructed Ash that no money was to be taken from the old man. This annoyed Ash, and he demanded that Mangal charge the man. The shop was running at a loss anyway. Mangal shook his head deferentially, saying that the man was a great soul and that his blessings were enough. Ash wasn't too pleased with this, but he kept quiet.

Ash began to grow curious about the old man. Sometimes, when it was windy, the man wore a loose, unwashed white cotton robe over his vest and pyjama, which reached just above his ankles. The robe, or *alkhalla*, had been patched up so many times in various places that it appeared to be made only of motley kerchiefs stitched together. The man also watched Ash occasionally, as he sat and shared words of wisdom with people at the tea shop adjacent to the beedi shop. A small crowd would settle down to hear him each time he came, much to Ash's amusement.

The man often carried an ektara and sang couplets, shlokas and bhajans as he talked with the group. He was quite tuneless and had a raspy voice. But he sang deeply meaningful bhajans. Ash wasn't very impressed initially, but he would overhear the talks as he sat in the beedi shop. One day, the old man sang a Meera bhajan that Ash recognized.

* * *

Vini began humming softly,

'*Bhaju man charan kamal avinaasi.*
Jetai deese dharan gagan bich,
tetai sab utthi jaasi.
Kaha bhayo teerath vrat keenhe,
kaha liye karvat Kaasi?
Iss dehi kaa garab naa karna
maati mein mil jaasi.
Yo sansaar chahar ki baaji,
saanjh pade utth jaasi.

Kaha bhayo hai bhagwa paheriya
ghar taj bhaye sanyasi?
Jogi hoy jugati nahi, jaani
ulati janam phir aasi,
Arj karun ablaa kar jorein,
Shyam tumhari dasi.
Meera ke prabhu Giridhar Nagar
kato jam ki phansi.'

Vini translated the bhajan for the mesmerized majlis,

'O mind, chant the name
of the Indestructible One with lotus feet.
Whatever you can see between earth and sky
will be destroyed.
Why do you perform pilgrimages and fasts?
Why do you go to die in Kashi?
Don't be proud of your body,
it will merge into dust.
This world is akin to a sporting of sparrows
that ends at dusk.
What's achieved by donning ochre robes
and leaving home to become an ascetic?
Wearing an ascetic's garb, unable to realize the truth,
you remain stuck in the net of rebirth.
Meera's liege, O royal mountain holder,
sever the death lord's noose.'

* * *

Ash gradually began to listen keenly to the man's
songs. He didn't really understand much, as the man

didn't pronounce the words very clearly. But there was something gentle and comforting in the way he spoke. One day, after the man had gone, Ash sought out one of the villagers who had been sitting near the old man and asked him about the song. The man was at sea; he said that he simply came and sat there whenever 'Baba' came. He didn't understand most of what was said. But he had faith that Baba was taking care of him. Ash shook his head incredulously.

The next time the old man came, Ash stood outside the beedi shop, a bit closer to the tea stall, in order to hear the man's words. Gradually, Ash began getting more interested in the man's words. Mangal noticed that Ash began leaving the shop unattended whenever the man came, but he never stopped Ash from doing so. The old man would talk about life, love and happiness most of the time. He spoke in very simple words, and he hardly gave any advice to anyone.

Ash often interacted with the man's devotees and was intrigued. They were simple, uneducated people from the village. They had great regard for the old man. Baba, they called him. No one knew his actual name.

One day, when the man came to collect beedis, Ash lit a beedi and gave it to him. The old man stared at Ash for a long time wordlessly as he smoked his beedi. He beckoned to Ash to come and sit with him and share a glass of sweet tea from the adjacent shop. Ash happily gulped down the tea. Soon, he and the man got chatting. The man spoke in a local dialect of Bangla. 'What is your name, béta?' he asked kindly.

'Ashwini Kumar, Babaji,' Ash replied.

'Ah! The healer to the gods! You have come here recently, isn't it so?' the old man asked.

'Yes, Babaji. I used to live in the city. But now I live with Mangal Dada.'

'Do you like it here? City dwellers don't enjoy village life too much. Don't you find it tough?' the man asked with a twinkle in his eyes.

'I have become used to it now, Babaji. Mangal Dada has been very kind to me,' Ash said, sighing softly.

'You are young, but you seem to have experienced a long life already. Have you had a difficult time?'

'Uh-huh.' Ash wasn't keen on opening up to the man. He was reticent, and the man didn't probe.

'We all go through testing times, béta. It is good that you have made it through. Come and sit with me in the gatherings, whenever possible. You will feel better,' the man said, looking into Ash's eyes. His gaze seemed to bore into Ash's soul. Ash felt disconcerted and tried to avert his eyes from the old man's piercing stare but couldn't. He felt engulfed in something warm and comfortable. There was an invisible force that kept his eyes locked into the man's eyes until the man nodded and smiled. Ash blinked. His eyes were watering, and he felt his heart pounding hard. He had never felt this kind of magnetic pull before.

Ash began to go and sit in the gatherings. He listened intently to the old man. He didn't ask questions, but he felt at peace whenever he attended the gathering. One day, after the gathering, as Ash lit a beedi for the old man, he decided to share his story. The old man listened quietly and nodded slowly throughout the narration. The sun was about to set when he finished. The old man didn't hurry him through his story even once, despite the difficulty he would have to face getting back to his forest home in the dark.

Once Ash ended his tale, the old man patted him on the back, and Ash felt a million tonnes lighter. Ash felt a strong bond was beginning to form between him and the man. He stood watching forlornly, as the old man shuffled his way back into the forest in the fading evening light.

A few weeks later, the man beckoned to Ash. 'Béta, how do you earn your living here?' the old man asked.

'Babaji, as you know, Mangal Dada has given me a place to stay and, in exchange, I work at his beedi shop. I do not have any other income,' Ash said.

'Hmm. Do you like working at the shop?'

'Um . . . It helps me pay Mangal Dada back for staying here Babaji. I had told him that we could expand the business, but he is happy with how things stand.'

The old man nodded slowly. He was quiet for a few minutes and then said, 'You like doing business, isn't it?'

'Yes, Babaji. I used to run large businesses earlier. I can help Mang- . . .'

'Would you like to make some money?' the man cut him off. 'Then, you can start your own business once again.'

Ash looked surprised. 'I . . . I would quite like that.'

'You would have to live with me at my hut in the forest. I am getting old now, and I need a young man like you to help me. I will pay you good money for this,' the man said seriously. 'Don't worry, I do have money to give you.' He smiled warmly. 'But I have one condition. You would not have any right to question me. I require complete obedience.'

Ash was a bit surprised. 'What kind of work could the old man have in his hut?' he wondered. 'Babaji, I would be really happy if I could earn a little money. I am confident that I can start a business with a small investment. But I need to talk to Mangal Dada before committing to you.'

'That would be the best thing to do Ashwini Béta.' The old man nodded approvingly as he got up to go.

Once the man left, Ash went and told Mangal about the offer. Mangal agreed immediately, 'You must go. It would be a real honour to serve the great soul.'

Ash decided to tell the old man that he was ready to work for him on his next visit. But he had no idea what was in store for him. Ash's entire life was about to transform once again.

* * *

Vini became quiet as he ended Ash's story for the day. The majlis, too, sat in silence. They were eager to hear more, but Vini was in a different place. His eyes were unfocused. He had a faraway look on his face and appeared to be lost in a daydream.

8

The Fight

The Aravalli Club was more of a banquet hall with a restaurant than the other way around. Actually, it wasn't even a club, but the name sounded exotic, and it had stuck. It had a beautiful lawn and good food. More importantly, it had a cosy feel. Jay's classmates met there regularly. In the past couple of years, he had hardly ever joined them.

When Jay arrived at the club, everyone else had already reached. The next day was Mahavir Jayanti, and the full moon had just risen. The ambience was marred by loud Punjabi hits being belted out at a marriage event that was happening on one end of the lawn. Jay saw his friends seated on plastic chairs in a circle drinking beer. He guessed that the food was the same as that being served in the marriage party. The fixed menu was economical for the caterers and gave visitors good value for their money.

'Hey, Jay. Good to see you!' said Raghav. Everyone greeted him, and Jay suddenly felt like a school kid once again. There were twelve of them in total. A couple of the classmates had begun balding and some had gained paunches. Jay couldn't see any women there.

Jay felt good meeting his old friends. Soon, they were all chatting as if they were still at school. Inane jokes were being cracked and childhood pranks were remembered fondly. Many of the friends were not well off, and the venue for the monthly meetings had been chosen carefully, so as not to hurt anyone's pride. The Aravalli Club was pretty reasonable and suited everyone's pocket.

The evening was going fine, and soon the topic shifted to wives and girlfriends. Inevitably, Jay's colourful past came up. He had been a Casanova at school, the envy of his classmates. Everyone was reminiscing about the fun they'd had at school. The drinks were flowing, and hot chicken tikka was being served. Jay was on his third whisky. The evening was going very well.

Jay was laughing and enjoying the attention when Chirag, the guy for whom the party had been thrown, asked, 'Hey, Jay, tell us about your wife. I am sure, women must have fallen over each other to get hitched with you!' Everyone laughed.

Jay shrugged it off. 'Far from it, Chirag. No such luck with me yet. Still very much a bachelor!'

But the others brought up his broken relationships. 'Jay, we are all getting old waiting for the big day. Every couple of years, we hear you are taking the plunge, but it's a damp squib. When will you become serious, man?' one guy said.

The group stood in the lawn, and the music blared on. Jay was feeling uncomfortable with the turn the conversation had taken, although it was all in good fun. He felt things were getting too personal. He wanted to get out of there.

'Jay can't make up his mind. He is always looking for someone better. Like the next iPhone!' one obviously drunk guy joked. Everyone laughed.

Jay was shocked to see Raghav laughing along with the others, and his eyes flashed angrily. He immediately turned defensive. He growled, 'This is different. I am in a serious relationship with Ritika.'

Raghav, who was also a bit drunk, spoke up. 'Serious my foot. Take it from me, Jay, she'll ditch you. She's screwing your happiness completely. She is not the right girl for you at all!'

A couple of other guys nodded, and suddenly Jay began to feel hounded. As if on cue, a waiter arrived with more drinks and chicken tikka, and everyone was distracted, to Jay's relief.

A few minutes passed. The music from the marriage party blared on, and most of the classmates were chatting in small groups now. Raghav had had a drink too many, and he didn't want to let go of this opportunity to say his piece. He came close to Jay and put his hand over Jay's shoulder. Raghav spoke earnestly, 'Jay, you're my best friend. Please listen to me for once, yaar. I think you just keep these girls around because you want to prove to everyone that you are a complete man who cannot fail at anything. You are fantastic at business, but you need to accept that your choice when it comes to girls is terrible. Each one of them used you and then betrayed you.'

Raghav's words were emphatic and came out in a torrent. By now, Jay was scowling. His face had darkened, and he had tensed up. Chirag and the others were watching them from afar, and Jay didn't like it at all—especially Raghav talking about Ritika in front of everyone. He shrugged off Raghav's hand.

Raghav knew Jay was getting agitated and tried to calm him down. 'Jay, you are the happiest when you are not with her. She's bad news, yaar. Don't get stuck with her. Please take things slo- . . .'

Thwack!

Raghav didn't see it coming. Jay's fist had hit him squarely on the jaw. He slipped and fell on the grass, slightly dazed. His ears were ringing. All his tipsiness vanished instantly, and he was up in a flash. Jay had already leaped at him, landing blows on his best friend and screaming expletives. The others realized that a fight had broken out and rushed to separate the two.

Raghav was a tough man. He had worked hard all his life and had never shied away from physical labour. He could give back as good as he got, if not better. He hardly felt Jay's blows. He instinctively swung his fists as he turned to face Jay and landed a few really hard punches on Jay's chin and face, and Jay fell down, groaning.

Raghav immediately tried to help him up, worried for him, as the other guys pulled them apart. The scuffle had happened really quickly; everything was over within a couple of minutes.

'DON'T TOUCH ME!' Jay shouted at the classmates who were trying to help him up. He angrily pushed them away as he got to his feet. Blinded with rage, Jay blew up. 'What have you all done with your lives? Nothing! All you do is come here every month and gossip like slum-dwelling women. Do something worthwhile. Look at me! I have done six multicrore projects so far! I make more money in a month than any of you can make in your entire life.'

Everyone was shell-shocked and started moving away from Jay, whose loud voice was echoing through the entire lawn. 'You all are bloody useless bums! I don't need your suggestions about whom to marry and what to do with my life! I have proved myself. I am far, far ahead of all of you today. Before making fun of anyone, try to be their equal!' Jay ranted on.

'I have made it big on my own. No one has helped me. Today, I can buy anything I want. Branded clothes, designer watches, cars. Anything. I travel business class. I meet ministers and top industrialists every day. Has any of you achieved even one percent of what I have?'

Jay turned towards Raghav. 'And you, Rags, you are a snake! I trusted you, and this is what you do to me! You have grown up eating the refuse from my house! How dare you laugh at me? Who do you think you are? Bloody backstabber!'

Jay wiped his bleeding lower lip with the back of his hand. He sneered at the whole group standing in shock in front of him. 'You all have a small-town mentality. You'll never be able to take any risks. It takes guts to become successful, my friends. And, you all are useless, bloody good-for-nothings.'

Saying this, Jay stormed off in a huff, leaving all his childhood friends aghast.

* * *

Jay reached the flat, but Ritika wasn't home. He cursed himself as he had forgotten his house keys in the hurry to leave for the mall. He called Ritika, and the phone rang until it disconnected on its own; she didn't pick up. Jay's lip was still bleeding, and he decided to go to his dad's place. He reached in less than ten minutes.

Jay walked in and his father saw his bloodied lip. Satish looked concerned. 'What happened, Jay?'

Jay didn't reply. Satish came close to him. Jay smelt of liquor. Satish frowned and once again demanded to know what had happened.

Jay said, 'Nothing happened.'

'Of course something happened. You don't get a split lip just like that, Jay! I haven't grown up in some ashram.' Satish was insistent. By now, Shubhra had rushed out. She let out a cry seeing Jay bleeding and immediately began fussing over him. 'What happened, béta?' she asked.

'I am sure he's been in a fight, Shubhra.' Satish glowered. 'Ask him.' Shubhra looked askance at Jay.

He let out a long breath. 'Dad's right. There was a fight. With Raghav.' Shubhra's eyes widened in shock. 'But Ma, it wasn't my fault. All the guys there ganged up against me.'

Satish opened his mouth to say something, but Shubhra gestured to him and he kept quiet. He turned, walked quickly into the dining room and pulled open the top drawer in a bureau next to the dining table. Rummaging through a wooden box, he pulled out a bunch of Band-Aids. He took one, shuffled back quickly and stuck it on Jay's split and swollen lower lip, while Jay stood awkwardly, avoiding eye contact.

'It's not too deep. Should be okay by morning. Have you eaten anything?' Satish asked as he pressed the ends of the plaster hard into Jay's cheek. Jay winced at the pressure but didn't reply. He simply shook his head.

Shubhra said, 'Go and have a bath, and come down for dinner.'

Jay nodded and meekly went up to his room. Satish followed him with his eyes, looking extremely concerned.

Dinner was a quiet affair. Good counsel prevailed, and no one was provoked. Jay found it difficult to eat with the Band-Aid on half his mouth, but Shubhra insisted. Satish gave him a Combiflam. He didn't protest. After dinner, Jay went up immediately and slept.

The next morning at breakfast, Shubhra had made Jay's favourite gobhi parathas with pudina raita and mango pickle. All through the meal, she kept calling Raghav, but his number was unavailable constantly.

Jay became annoyed seeing his mother trying Raghav's number again and again. Finally, he told her, 'Just stop it, Ma! Don't waste your time on that ungrateful snake!'

Satish stared at Jay. 'What happened yesterday, Jay? Why did Raghav hit you?'

Jay was frowning. 'I don't want to talk about it, Dad. Suffice to say that I misread the guy completely.

I too gave it back to him. I thought he was my friend, but he is not.'

Shubhra said, 'He's your best friend, Jay. You should sort things out, béta. Please call him.'

Jay sneered and said that Raghav was getting too big for his boots. Raghav seemed to have blocked all communication with Jay and his family.

Satish retorted, 'It can't be one-sided, Jay. I know both of you very well. You've grown up together. He's like a brother to you. You must have said something that upset him.'

Jay was about to reply, but Satish carried on, 'This is typical of you, Jay. Your ego comes up and you start getting argumentative. And then, things start turning ugly. I don't want to know why you fought, béta. But he's your only friend. You don't *have* any other friends. I think you should behave like mature adults and patch up.'

Jay couldn't control himself any longer. 'What's your problem, Dad? Why do you keep taking his side? I am a grown man. I run my own business. I know what I am doing! Rags *was* a friend. We *had* good times. He *has been* a good pal. But we gave him a lot, too. *I* gave him a lot more than he gave me! And now, I am done with that snake in the grass!'

Angry at Satish for siding with Raghav, Jay stormed off and went to his bedroom to try to get some sleep. The entire previous evening—from his argument with Ritika to his fight with Raghav, and this morning's altercation with his father—played in his head for a long time. He kept tossing and turning until sleep came to him.

He didn't wake up until Ritika called him around afternoon, and he quickly left for Hauz Khas.

9

Ajaat

'Speak to us of loss. Why does losing someone hurt so much?' a man at the majlis asked Vini.

'Loss isn't such a bad thing. When we are attached to things, we don't want them to change. But the reality is, deep in our hearts we already know that nothing will last forever, and we hope against hope that things won't change. When someone we really love is taken from us, we are saddened. Although we know that we cannot bring back the past, we ache and hurt because we want their comforting presence in our lives forever. It is very important to grieve when we lose someone. Grieving makes us tender and brings us close to our heart. Different people grieve differently.'

'Some people think that grieving makes them weak. They suppress their pain and become hardened,' someone at the majlis observed.

Vini nodded in agreement. 'Sometimes loss can make us hateful and bitter. We can either grow into beautiful people through loss, or we can become bitter and angry. It is a choice we have to make ourselves,'

Vini explained gently. 'Ash had gone through so much loss in his life, and it changed him. But as time passed, old patterns began surfacing. Ash was at a crucial juncture of his life . . .'

* * *

There were subtle signs that only an awakened soul could read. The old man knew that time was short. Ash was at a crucial juncture of his life. He was on the verge of falling back into the vagaries of the material world. But, if pushed in the right direction, he could attain great spiritual heights. The old man knew that the push wasn't going to be pleasant for Ash.

The next time the man came for his beedis, Ash told him that he was ready to work for him, as he wanted to save some money and begin a business. The old man nodded slowly and told him to go head back to the forest with him that evening. 'But remember, Ashwini, you will have to do exactly what I tell you.'

'I am sure I will manage, Babaji. Your work can't be too tough. Let me go and collect my things,' Ash said.

The man smiled gently and left for the gathering. When he finished, Ash was waiting with a duffle bag in his hand. He was quite proud of the fact that he had been able to fit all his worldly possessions into one bag. Mangal stood slightly behind him with folded hands. He was happy for Ash. The old man saw them and nodded. He gave his ektara to Ash to carry and began shuffling back towards the forest. Ash slung his bag over his shoulder and followed him. They walked quietly for some time, and all Ash could hear was the sound of their feet and the old man's laboured breathing.

'May I know your name?' Ash asked the man.

'Eh?' The man stopped and turned his head to hear better. Ash realized that he was probably a bit hard of hearing.

'Your name. I mean, it cannot be Baba. You must have a name,' Ash said.

'Oh,' the man wheezed. 'Call me anything you want to. It hardly matters what you call me.'

'But I am sure you have a name, Baba,' Ash persisted.

The old man sighed and said, 'Ajaat. Call me Ajaat. That is a good name.' His face crinkled into a smile.

'Ajaat. That's an unusual name. What does it mean?'

'It means "the Unborn". We all are Ajaat, béta. No one's ever born, no one ever dies,' he said as he sat down on a rock to catch his breath. 'Light a beedi for me.'

Ash did as told. Ajaat smoked in silence, looking westwards at the reddish evening sunlight filtering through leafy trees. He took his ektara from Ash and began to sing softly:

'Jaat gelo jaat gelo, bole eki ajob karkhana!
Sultyu kuje keu nai, raaji sobi dekhi ta na na na.
Asbar kaa-le ki jaat chile ese tumi ki jaat nile
Ki jaat hoba jabar kaa-le se kotha bhebe bolona.
Bramhon chondal chamor muchi
ek jolei sab hoi go suchi.

Dekhe suune hoi na ruchi jome to-o kakeo charbena.
Gopone je beshyar bhaat khay
tate dhormer ki khoti hoi.
Lalon bole, jaat kare koi e bhrom to gelo o naa.'

* * *

Vini sang Lalon Fakir's baul song for the majlis and then translated it,

'Caste has disappeared. Identity has dissolved.
What a strange factory this is!
None are keen to do the supreme work,
I see everyone saying "no no, not that".
What was your caste before birth?
What caste did you obtain once you got here?
What will your caste be when you depart?
Think and then tell me about this.
Brahmins, outcastes, tanners and cobblers,
all are purified by the very same water.
Seeing and hearing cannot trigger keen desire,
death will not spare anyone.
When someone enjoys being fed by whores secretly,
how can religion be the loser?
Lalon says, the misconception
what caste really is, hasn't really gone away.'

Vini continued, 'Ash and Ajaat had been walking through the hilly forest for almost two hours. Ash was quite surprised at Ajaat's stamina. He kept trudging along doggedly, despite smoking beedis. Ash was out of breath all through the way. Ajaat's hut was on a high ground, and a dirt path led up to it . . .'

* * *

Immediately on arriving, Ajaat took some water in a cracked blue plastic mug from an old drum placed outside the hut and washed his face, hands and feet. He indicated that Ash should do the same. He gave Ash his *gamchha*, a thin white-and-red cotton towel, to wipe himself. Ash followed Ajaat inside the hut.

The thatched hut was large and empty except for a *khaat*, or a wooden cot, placed on one end. Beside the door, a kerosene lantern was burning with a very low flame. Ash guessed that someone had left after lighting the lamp just a few minutes before they arrived. There was a cooking space with a *chulha*, a stove made of mud and bricks, at the far end. A small window opened on a small vegetable garden behind the hut. Some clothes hung on a long, drooping clothesline close to the foot of the bed separating the cooking area from the sleeping area. There was a worn brownish mosquito net hanging above the cot with its edges thrown over the top. Ash noticed that the ceiling was made of thatched straw and the floor was covered in dried cow dung. The room was swept clean, and the bed linen was neatly folded. On the right, Ash saw a *chataai*, or mat, where Ajaat had placed his ektara. He guessed that Ajaat possibly sang or meditated on the chataai. To the right of the entrance, there was a large round clay *ghada*, or pot, filled with drinking water.

It was placed on a black, three-pronged metal stand. The pot was covered with a dented aluminium plate and a brass *lota*, a small tumbler, was placed upside down on it. Ash guessed that the locals looked after Ajaat's basic needs and took care of the maintenance of his hut.

Ajaat gave Ash some food out of a couple of blackened utensils. Ash was ravenous and ate hungrily. Ajaat watched with slight amusement as he ate his own meal very slowly and deliberately. Ash had finished nearly three times the amount of food Ajaat ate, before the old man was even halfway through his meal. He could hear jackals howling in the forest as he sat and waited for Ajaat to finish his meal in the semi-darkness of the lantern's light.

After the meal, Ajaat got up slowly, and went outside to wash his plate and the other utensils. Ash followed him and cleaned his plate as well. Ajaat showed Ash the latrine and bathing area, at the base of their small hillock, in the opposite direction from where they had come up to the hut. Both of them went there, with Ajaat holding the flickering lantern. Ash used the toilet gingerly after Ajaat and got back to the hut carefully, following the old man. Ajaat then gave Ash a blanket to spread on the floor close to his own cot. He told Ash to rest and start work the next day.

Ajaat woke Ash up in the cold darkness of pre-dawn. It was colder in the forest than in the village, Ash realized. Ajaat had already finished his ablutions, and after dispatching Ash for his, the old man began to stretch; it was followed by prayer and meditation.

By the time the sun rose, a tribal couple had appeared and begun cleaning the perimeter of the hut. Ajaat instructed Ash to pick up chopped wood lying at the front entrance to the hut and to stack it at the back. He had extremely strict rules of work, and made Ash repeat the stacking three times at different places around the hut. He then told Ash to eat some breakfast, before telling him to remove weeds from the garden at the back of the hut. He wasn't satisfied and made Ash dig the same vegetable patch five times. By now, Ash was getting exasperated.

Within hours, Ash began to have arguments with Ajaat. 'Why can't you make up your mind, Babaji? Please tell me once what you want me to do, and I will do it. What's the point of making me do the same thing again and again? I could have done so much more during this time!'

Ajaat didn't reply and called Ash for lunch, which they both had in silence. After the frugal lunch, Ajaat said, 'Ashwini, I had placed one simple condition on you. You haven't been able to fulfil it on your first day itself. You can follow whatever I say without asking questions, or you can leave.'

Ash was sullen when he went back to work. He worked in silence for three hours, without even looking at Ajaat, who would periodically examine Ash's handiwork and tell him to redo things. Ajaat was very particular about things that Ash found nonsensical, but Ash kept his own counsel. As the sun started to go down, Ajaat told him to stop work for the day. Ash now told Ajaat that he had had enough and didn't

wish to work for him any more. He wanted Ajaat to
pay him for the day.

Ajaat's face was expressionless. He simply said,
'Fine. Go inside the hut, on the right side, near
the chataai you will find a *sandook*. Open it and
take whatever you think is enough for your day's
payment.'

Ash went inside and located the wooden chest,
which he hadn't noticed the previous evening. It
wasn't locked. When Ash opened it, he was aghast.
There was a pile of antique silver coins in the chest
worth lakhs of rupees. Even a single coin was worth
more than a month's pay for the work Ash had done.
Next to the pile lay crumpled Rs 50 and Rs 100 notes,
and some gold jewellery. Ash spotted some precious
and semi-precious stones. Shocked beyond belief, he
picked up a Rs 100 note and closed the sandook.
When he came outside, Ajaat was strumming his
ektara.

> *'Sattya kaje keu nai raaji,*
> *sobi dekhi ta na na na.'*

Ash stood still, wanting to say something. Ajaat simply
smiled and indicated that he should leave. Ash slung
his duffle bag on his shoulder and hurriedly left before
the sun set.

Predictably, Ash, who had no clue of the route out of
the woods, got completely lost in the darkening forest.
It soon began to drizzle, and in the cold and clammy
twilight, Ash wandered on to a ridge and slipped down

a slope. His duffle bag flew off his shoulder and rolled away. He cried out as he fell into a deep opening on the hillside.

The walls of the angular cave were slippery with moss, and it was quite cold inside. Ash desperately tried to claw his way out of the cave as it started getting dark. He began shouting for help. Within a few minutes, Ash saw a tribal man peeking inside. He spoke rapidly in some local language that Ash couldn't understand. He indicated that Ash should throw his shirt and trackpants up to him. Ash guessed that the man wanted to make a rope out of them and help him climb out to safety. He undressed quickly and threw his clothes up to the man, who said something rapidly and disappeared from view.

Ash stood in his underwear, waiting for the man to throw the makeshift rope down to him. Ash went hoarse calling out to the man, until he realized that the man had disappeared with his clothes. He screamed in frustration standing in the clammy cave, almost naked, in the chilly night. Terribly cold and frightened, Ash sat down in the darkness, hearing the crickets and howling jackals. He huddled next to something soft and slowly began to get warm. Almost immediately, the tiredness from the hard day of work took him over and he fell asleep.

Next morning, as day broke, Ash woke up to chirping birds, completely disoriented. His body was stiff and cold. As daylight filtered into the cave, he saw that it was a dead jackal that he had been huddled against. He leaped away, crying out in fear.

Ash screamed for help, scared, thirsty and hungry. It took him hours to claw out of the cave using broken twigs and some sharp stones. He even lost his slippers as he clambered out. Bruised, scratched and muddy, he stood barefoot outside the cave in his underwear. His skin was stained moss-green, brown and black, and he desperately began looking for a way out of the forest. Ash wandered in circles for hours, until he recognized the far-off hillock where Ajaat's hut stood. It was past noon by the time he found his way back to Ajaat's hut.

When he entered, Ajaat was sitting in the sun. He looked at Ash expressionlessly for a few moments before breaking into a guffaw. Ash sheepishly told him what had happened. Ajaat listened kindly and told Ash to have a bath with the sun-warmed water from the drum. He gave Ash leftovers of his half-eaten morning meal, and one of his vests and a pyjama to wear. He gently told Ash, 'You have suffered a lot, béta. Rest a while, and then you can follow me out of the forest in the afternoon, when I go to get my beedis. I am sure Mangal will be happy to have you back.'

Ash sat for a while in silence. Then, he said quietly, 'Babaji, I am really sorry for my stupid behaviour yesterday. I apologize for my arrogance. I know I don't deserve your grace. Mangal Dada had told me not to leave your side, but I have been foolish. Please forgive me. Can you please give me another chance? Please take me back. I do not want any money from you. I want to learn how you can give it away so easily. How have you become completely detached from material things? Ajaatji, I want to learn that truth which has set you free!'

Ajaat was compassionate and agreed. He acknowledged that maybe he had been too hard on Ash on his very first day. That evening, Ajaat didn't go to the village. He sat with Ash by his side and sang softly,

> 'Soiee pandit, soiee paarkhi, soiee sant sujaan.
> Soiee suur sachet, so soiee subhat pramaan.
> Soiee gyaanii, soiee gunii jan, soiee daataa dhyaani.
> Tulasii jaake chit bhaiee, raag dvesh kii haani.'

> 'They are adepts, they are connoisseurs,
> they are saints and good men.
> They are fully aware,
> and exhibit real evidence of awakening.
> They are wise, they are qualified,
> they are true givers and remain contemplative.
> Tulsidas proclaims, they are the ones
> who have annihilated attachments and aversions
> from their entire being.'

That evening, Ash slept well.

* * *

Vini concluded the majlis for that evening. He got up and slowly walked away.

10

Maelstrom

'*Get in, get in!*' *Get in, get in!*

Jay is running fast. The last bogie is right next to him. But the door is too high. He will have to jump very high to get inside.

His hands feel heavy. The two suitcases seem to be stuck to the ground. He turns to his right and sees that Ritika is sitting on one, laughing loudly. Suddenly, she is on his left, squatting on the other suitcase, wailing loudly, grasping at Jay, not letting him move. Mascara pours out of her eyes in torrents and begins covering her face, the suitcase and everything around. The black, tarry gook begins flowing towards him, and he wants to leap backwards, but he can't let go of his grip on the suitcase.

Jay looks up. Hooda is standing at the bogie's door. He is the guard. He has a huge, brightly coloured whistle which throws out fake-looking Rs 2000 notes whenever he blows into it. He gloats and grins as he keeps shouting, 'Get in, get in!' with the rhythmic beat of the train's couplings.

Jay decides to take the leap, but his feet are stuck in the tarry mascara. He stumbles and falls as the train rushes away, making a rhythmic buzzing sound.
Buzz, buzz . . . buzz, buzz . . .

Jay's phone was buzzing continuously, and he got up with a start. The sun was streaming through the curtains. He looked at his phone. Four missed calls. Pam had been calling. It was 8.30 a.m. He had slept like a log. He turned and saw that Ritika was still in deep sleep. She snored softly. A strand of her hair was on her cheek. Jay smiled and gently tucked it behind her ear. He went out of the room and called Pam.

'Hi, Pam. Sorry, I overslept.'

'Jay, switch on the news. There's major chaos. The government has fallen. Indian National Social Party has withdrawn support. They have a floor test next week.'

'So?' Jay was still groggy.

'So, our project is in trouble, Jay! Hooda's brother-in-law is no longer the minister!'

'Hell!' Jay leaped up, wide awake. 'Where are you, Pam? Let's meet at the office at 9.30.' He raced to get ready, heart thumping, and took off for the office before Ritika awoke.

'Jay, this was really so sudden! Hooda needs to be contacted immediately. Shyam and Girish don't know about this yet.' Pam was panicky. Her husband, Arjun, had heard the news as he was jogging in the morning. He was worried as he had given Pam Rs 2.5 crore for Hooda's bribe.

Jay calmed Pam down. He said, 'The first thing we need to do is inform our partners, Pam. They trusted us with their money. As did your husband. Then, we need to start making calls.'

Calling up Shyam and Girish had been an unpleasant task. They had absolutely no understanding of the way ALSOL functioned. They saw Jay as the guy they had given money to, and he had been bringing them good returns. That kept them happy.

All through the next week, Jay tried to contact Hooda and Sagar, but their phones remained switched off. Jay even went to the hotel where he had met Hooda, but nobody could help him. Going to the police was out of the question.

The government lost the floor test ten days later. The opposition cobbled up numbers and immediately came to power. To Jay's utter shock, ALSOL was summarily informed that the amusement park project had been scrapped.

Sharma refused to meet Jay. On the solitary occasion when he took Jay's call, before blocking his number, he casually shrugged everything off saying, 'What money? I don't know what you are talking about.' Since there was no money trail, the bribe money was gone without a trace.

In the next few days, Jay tried to put together as many small projects as he could. He was constantly running from one meeting to another and preparing presentations at the office whenever he was free. He hardly got time at home or to socialize. His pride was hurt, and he wanted to recover the losses quickly through other projects. Yet, he sincerely wanted to make ALSOL a respectable company. So he didn't want to take up projects that wouldn't help build their brand image. Unfortunately, when one is in a rush to recover losses, one has to make compromises. Not all projects coming ALSOL's way at this point were respectable and above board. Jay was constantly grappling with the dilemma whether he should make up for the losses by taking up low-quality projects. Soon, Jay started becoming sleep-deprived and irritable.

Ritika sensed Jay's stress and decided that she needed to move quickly. She began to rush away to meet Timmy and Puja, and soon began dating Sahil on the quiet. Earlier, whenever she and Jay were at home, they used to argue. But now, she was walking on thin ice. Nowadays, Jay refused to go anywhere and slept off whenever he got the chance. Ritika didn't push him too much. He didn't stop her from going out on her own, and she was holding on to the platinum credit card he had given her. She was clear that she needed Jay and the comforts provided by him, until she was certain of Sahil. She didn't want to provoke Jay too much right now and consciously avoided escalating their rows. This came as a boon in disguise for Jay, who thought Ritika was being uncharacteristically considerate to him and had changed for the better.

But Jay did feel that something was amiss. He tried to pinpoint what could have triggered this change for the better in Ritika, but he had too much on his plate right now, and he stored this thought away for the time being. Why rock the boat? For now, he needed peace and quiet when he was back from work, and Ritika was obligingly giving him space. He saw her busy on her phone, chatting and smiling away, most of the time. He guessed it was Puja and didn't inquire any further. She was letting him be, and he was relieved that he could catch up with the rare luxury of sleep.

But Ritika was the least of Jay's troubles. The wise ones say that our troubles come in bunches, and Jay's problems had just begun.

Within a few weeks, one of the building projects that Jay had taken up for a local businessman came under the scanner of the municipal corporation and was partially demolished before ALSOL had been paid all the money. Soon, two more projects were in the doldrums. Things were going downhill rapidly.

A month after the disappearance of Hooda, Girish had his tenth marriage anniversary party at a small hotel. Jay asked Ritika to come to the party with him, but, having already made her own clandestine plans for the evening, she flatly refused, calling the venue a downmarket, seedy joint where she wouldn't even wish to be seen dead. Since it had been a particularly gruelling day, Jay didn't insist and went off directly from the office with Pam.

The venue wasn't as bad as Ritika had made it out to be. The function was at a banquet hall, where many of Girish's relatives and friends were sitting in rows, on chairs covered in white satin cloth, facing the stage, which was brightly lit up with halogen lights. There was Indian classical instrumental music playing softly and the room smelt of jasmine. Liveried waiters carried a wide variety of tandoori snacks and a concoction of ice cream and Fanta. Pam saw Jay looking a bit overwhelmed and said, 'I am sure there's a bar somewhere.'

'I hope so!' said Jay, looking around for a place to sit down.

Girish and his wife were sitting on a plush, gold and maroon, velvety sofa on the stage, and people were lined up on one side, walking up in small groups to greet Girish and take the obligatory photograph.

Jay had to wait his turn to meet Girish too. Jay spotted a waiter carrying a tray with whisky, ice and soda, and beckoned to him. He quickly downed a couple of whiskies and started feeling pleasantly numb. He went and met Girish half an hour later, on stage. Girish told him that he and Shyam wanted to meet Jay as soon as Girish came off the stage.

Twenty minutes later, all four partners were sitting together in a private room on one side of the hall. Jay had downed an additional couple of whiskies by then and was feeling a warm buzz in his head. Pam looked concerned.

Shyam said, 'Jay, what is the plan now? How do we recover our losses?'

Jay said, 'I am trying hard, Shyam. We need time to work it out. It's not going to be that simple.'

Girish chipped in, 'Jay Bhai, for us this is simple business. We have trusted you with a lot of money. How do you plan to get it back?'

'We need some big projects where we can make good profit, Girish. It's not easy to make ten–twelve crore so fast.' Jay sounded insistent, and his voice was slurring slightly.

Girish looked at Shyam. It appeared that there was something they had already discussed among themselves before calling this impromptu meeting—something Jay knew nothing about. Girish said, 'We should try to recoup our losses through each and every project that comes our way, Jay. We cannot afford to let go of anything right now. Why have you refused to look at the three contracts that came to ALSOL through Kanshi and Pandey?'

Jay felt annoyed as Girish was trying to enter into his domain. The three projects that Kanshi and Pandey, two corrupt middlemen, had brought to him were dubious and could mean trouble. 'I don't . . .'

Shyam interrupted him. 'Girish is right, Jay. Through these projects, ALSOL would recover all the losses quickly.'

'The projects don't fit ALSOL's brand image, Shyam,' Jay said.

Shyam said, 'Jay, you know we are here for the profit only. I really don't care about the brand or the image. I am with you till I get profitable returns on my investment. You have run the company well so far, and we have been getting good returns. But now, we have to recover our ten crore immediately.'

Girish backed him, 'Jay Bhai, money is money. I want my three-crore investment back, and so does Shyam Bhai.'

Pam had to pitch in before Jay ruffled their feathers any more. 'Shyam, Girish,' she said. 'Jay is really doing his best. We want to do good projects because our good work gets us more business. One project fails, and we will be out of the market. There's a lot of competition, as you very well know. We have to be careful, otherwise we won't get any work in the future. Those three projects are unsafe. We can get into trouble.'

Jay was pretty high by now. 'Please don't teach me how to run the company, Shyam. I am working on this, and I will find a way out. I have given you so much profit every year. You have made shops and bought cars and houses! You have gone on holidays abroad while I work my ass off! And what do I get in return? Your demands? You both are the limit!'

Shyam was looking upset now. 'Jay, I think . . .'

Things would have got very ugly, but Pam intervened. 'Shyam, I think we can talk about this tomorrow. Right now, Jay needs to get home.'

'No, I don't, Pam. I want . . .' Jay slurred as Pam pulled him out of the room towards the exit.

'Jay, please, just shut up for now,' Pam hissed as they quickly went through the crowded banquet hall. No one really paid any attention as everyone was busy lining up for the sumptuous buffet. Pam called her driver on the phone, and her SUV was waiting for them before they reached outside. She quickly pushed a protesting Jay into the vehicle and instructed the driver to take Jay back to his home in Defence Colony.

11

Blossoming

'What is devotion?' questioned someone at the majlis.

'It is the highest blossoming of love,' Vini replied.

'And what is love?' asked another.

'Your very existence,' Vini said.

'Speak to us of love,' the majlis implored.

'All love arises out of your love for yourself. If you do not love yourself, how will you love another? How deeply do you love yourself? Where do you go to find how to love yourself? The way back home is a journey of finding love.

'Have you faced those parts of yourself that you do not like revisiting? You will find your home there. Have you kissed those unloved parts of you hidden away to avoid looking at them, because they fill you with disgust and hurt? You'll find your love there. Have you swum through the black and tarry sea filled with putrefying thoughts that make you cringe? Memories of incidents that make you feel unclean and nauseated? That's where you will find your freedom.

'When you begin to love all your unloved, rejected, cracked and broken pieces, you'll become whole. To be whole and complete, you must embrace all of yourself. The lovable and the unlovable. Completely, absolutely, totally.

'In this absolute acceptance, you will disappear forever. Even the parts that you like about yourself will be annihilated. There will be nothing left. No good, no bad. Nothing at all. That's the price of love that is total and absolute,' Vini said quietly.

'Is such a love possible?' the majlis wondered.

Vini nodded. 'Yes, it is. But, for such love you must be prepared to die. *It requires great courage to be ready to die, so that you can come alive.* You will only find yourself when you lose yourself completely. Like water that has completely disappeared in sandalwood paste and lost its own identity.

'Prabhuji, tum chandan, hum pani,
jaaki ang ang baas samaani.
Prabhuji, tum ghan, ban hum mora,
jaise chitwat chand chakora.
Prabhuji, tum moti, hum dhaga,
jaise sone milat suhaga.
Prabhuji, tum deepak hum baati,
jaaki jyoti barai dini raati.
Prabhuji, tum swami, hum dasa,
aisi bhakti karai Raidasa.

'Lord, you are sandalwood, I am water,
In every part of me your fragrance permeates.

Lord, you are rain clouds,
I have become a dancing peacock,
Like a chakora bird yearning for the moon.
Lord, you are the pearls, I am the unseen string,
Just as borax mixed in gold makes it shine.
Lord, you are the glowing lamp,
I am the burning wick
Whose brightness waxes day and night.
Lord, you are the master, I am the servant,
This is the way your devotee Raidas worships you.'

* * *

Ajaat was compassionate with Ash and explained the reason for repeatedly making him work on the same tasks. 'Son, there are deep-rooted habits that have formed in you over lifetimes. You need to get rid of them through certain actions. Just as we go to a doctor when we have a stomach ache, and he prescribes medicine, so we also need someone to give us medication to transform us. You have come to me, béta, and my medicine is bitter. You need to take it for a very long time, and you cannot stop until I say so. You will not like it, but it will surely heal you. That's my promise.'

Ash was filled with gratitude and said, 'You are my guru. I will do whatever you say, Ajaatji.'

Ajaat nodded and sat in contemplation. After a few minutes he said, 'The tribals need to study and learn about many things. You can work for their betterment.'

'I can teach them whatever I know,' Ash said.

'No, you will not teach them. Not yet. Right now, you will build them a school,' Ajaat said. 'Single-handedly. With your bare hands. There . . .'

Ajaat looked across the undulating forest land, pointing at a patch of land on a hillside a few hundred metres away. Ash stood looking at him, and towards the thickly wooded patch, in shock. He bit his lip as he felt the familiar resistance beginning to build up once more. Ajaat must be joking, he thought, but when he looked at Ajaat, he saw the old man watching him seriously. He wanted to say that Ajaat was crazy. He didn't know what he was saying, but his throat had suddenly become dry, and all that came out was a meek croak. 'As you wish, Ajaatji.'

That afternoon, Ash went to examine the patch of land and realized what a mammoth task this was going to be. But, as the days went by, building the school became an obsession. He would get up at the crack of dawn and plan his day meticulously. He had decided that he would also take care of Ajaat's hut. He spent time patching it up and cleared the weeds from the back garden. He brought seeds from the villages and planted them, both in the kitchen garden and in the area around the school. Within six months, Ash had beautified Ajaat's hut and the latrines, and he had even designed a solar water-heating system.

It had taken Ash a while to fall into a rhythm at Ajaat's hut. Life was hard, but his mind was calmer, and he felt rejuvenated. Then, one day, he suddenly realized that he had turned thirty-five years old. Three years had passed since that man had swallowed the cyanide pill at his birthday party. He and Ajaat would go to Mangal's village, where they spent the afternoon with the villagers. Ash would accompany Ajaat as he sang his songs, and he even sang a few of his own.

Ash now had a trimmed beard and looked wiry. His skin was tanned, and his body looked well-toned. His feet were becoming calloused. His palms had become rough from working with his hands all the time. He dressed in similar attire as Ajaat. He looked calm and worked quietly, happy with the same tasks he had so vehemently disliked when he first came to Ajaat. The school was coming up well, and Ash had to wait for the monsoon rains to end before beginning work again. The land had been smoothened, and a perimeter fence was up already. Ajaat was happy to see Ash's sincerity, but he neither praised nor criticized Ash. Some locals and villagers offered Ash help, but he refused categorically, saying, 'This is by my guru's *aagya*. These are his orders. I will do this all myself.'

Ajaat never taught Ash anything, but soon, as the school started coming up, Ash began realizing deep truths on his own.

One day, Ash came from the school to take Ajaat with him to the village. Ajaat lay in his bed, coughing. Ash wanted to call a village doctor, who was from Médecins Sans Frontières. Ajaat shook his head. He said, 'This cough isn't going to go away, béta. The beedis are taking their toll. You have to go to the village and conduct the *satsang* today.'

Ash sat down on the floor, next to Ajaat's cot. He didn't want to leave Ajaat's side, but the old man insisted. Ash said that he felt unsure of being able to handle the satsang all alone.

'You go and sit there, béta. Do not worry. I am there with you. *Just be as you are*,' Ajaat whispered as he put his hand on Ash's shoulder.

Ash left reluctantly. His mind was only on Ajaat. When he reached the village, Ash wanted to explain that Ajaat was unwell, and he needed to get back. But an unseen force seemed to gently guide him to the seat where Ajaat usually sat.

Ash sat down and closed his eyes, remembering Ajaat. He felt his guru's hand on his head. Tears flowed down his face as he sang a song of Amir Khusrau that talked of the pain of separation from the divine, strumming his ektara,

> *'Sun li hamre jiyaraa ki peerh,*
> *ankhiyaan se bahe hai neer.*
> *Kaahe ko byaahe bides?*
> *Arre lakhi baabul more, kaahe ko byaahe bides?*
> *Hum to baabul tore, bele ki kaliyaan,*
> *ghar-ghar maange jaaye.*
> *Arre lakhi baabul more, kaahe ko byaahe bides?*
> *Hum to baabul tore aangan ki chiraiyaan,*
> *chuge, piye, udd jaaye.*
> *Arre lakhi baabul more, kaahe ko byaahe bides?*
> *Hum to baabul tore, khuunte ki gaiyyaan,*
> *jit haanko hak jaaye.*
> *Arre lakhi baabul more, kaahe ko byaahe bides?'*

'Listen, I implore thee, to the ache in my heart,
as tears flow from my eyes.

Why have you married me off into a foreign land?
O wealthy father mine!
We are flower-buds from the vine in your garden,
wanted in every home.
O wealthy father mine,
why have you married me off into a foreign land?
We are just birds from your courtyard,
pecking, drinking and flying away.
O wealthy father mine,
why have you married me off into a foreign land?
We are simply your cows tied to stakes,
readily going wherever you drive us.
O wealthy father mine,
why have you married me off into a foreign land?'

'With Babaji's grace,' Ash said, 'I have begun to understand the intricate ways that karma has worked in my life. Every action has a repercussion, and all of us have to work through our karmas. If we work selflessly, with guru's grace, our karmas are gradually cleansed. This school is not just a building, it is a temple being built through me by Babaji.'

With Ajaat's blessings, the school began functioning in its first year itself. It had just eight children, and Ash taught them for a couple of hours every day, before continuing with the construction. It took two more years for Ash to complete the structure to his satisfaction. He had used wood and stone to build a large thatched central hall and six classrooms. All around the school structure ran a covered corridor. Ash had also cleared out a large area for a playground. In its second year, a teacher joined Ash, and thirty-five new students took admission. The school building had taken three years to complete, and by the fifth year it had 126 students and three teachers. Ash began handling administrative tasks, slowly receding to the background, and in its sixth year, the school began receiving donations and grants from various trusts.

By now, Ajaat was finding it difficult to move around. He had started encouraging Ash to hold satsangs on his own. Ash spoke of his own realizations. 'There is a divine power that is running our lives. It is the same power that makes the earth go around the sun. It is the same power that allows us to take our next breath. Who pulls in this breath? The breath leaves on its own accord. Who lets it leave? It is a power that is vast and beyond comprehension.' Ash was humbled at the vastness of creation and realized that all this was by the grace of Ajaat. He started going into long periods of silence.

As time passed, Ash became joyful and more at peace with himself. His words were soft and precise. He sang songs of many saints and traditions, as they touched him deeply. He sang beautifully, and always from his heart, in the presence of Ajaat. Often, the local villagers, including Mangal, came to listen to him.

'When you desire nothing and you are at the feet of your guru, you are blessed with the greatest treasures,' Ash told the villagers.

The day arrived when Ash came to know that Mangal had passed away. He went to pay his respects to his benefactor's family. They saw Ash as a great soul and treated him as their guide and teacher. Ash continued to conduct the gatherings at the tea stall beside the beedi shop. He took beedis for Ajaat and toothpaste for himself. He smiled when Mangal's son refused to take money, remembering his earliest days at the same shop. He blessed the boy and left, realizing how far he had come since those days, nearly ten years ago.

'*Karam ki gati nyaari, santon!*'

'Strange are the workings of karma, O wise ones!'

One day, Ajaat called Ash and made him sit on the chataai in their hut. They sat quietly for a long time. Ash saw Ajaat looking into nothingness, completely self-absorbed. His body had become frail and bent. Almost all his teeth were gone. He was nearly blind and completely deaf in one ear. But his face glowed with peace. Ash noticed his stubble and noted that he had to give the old man a shave the next day, when Ash bathed him.

Ash heard Ajaat's laboured breathing as he felt his own eyes close. Instantly, he went blank.

He felt that he was being sucked into himself. He realized that he was zooming backwards into his own head at a breakneck pace.

It was a vast emptiness without anything at all.

He had lost all awareness of the body. He had no form.

He had no thoughts.

He didn't know who or what he was.
He had no name, no form.
But he knew that he was.
He knew that he existed.
There was a sudden flash of blue, and his back gave a sharp jerk. A whiplash of tingling electricity hit the base of his skull.
His body awareness was back as suddenly as it had disappeared.
An indescribably pleasurable shockwave began to rise up from the base of his spine.
He felt his entire body tightly gripped in something like a huge and immensely powerful fist.
He had been seized by god, and he was being shaken like a rag doll. He had no control at all.
He stopped resisting and let go completely.
Wave upon wave of bliss rose through him and exploded in warm, honey-like rivulets inside his skull, rolling down his entire being.
Every atom of his existence was radiating a golden glow.
He lost awareness once again.
Eons passed. The world was reborn. He was reborn . . .

After an indeterminate time, Ajaat's eyes flickered, and he beckoned to Ash with a long and raspy 'Hmm'. Ash took a few moments to come out of his meditation and opened his eyes. He saw Ajaat had his right hand raised to bless him. Ash bent his head forward. Ajaat placed his palm on Ash's head and said softly, '*Ashwini is no more. You have been weaved afresh by the grace of the divine. From today onwards, you are Vini.'*

Agyaana timiraandhasya gyaanaanjana shalaakayaa.
Chakshurunmiilitam yena tasmai shri gurave namah.

The One who has removed
the pitch-black blindness of ignorance,
With the collyrium of the deepest wisdom.
The One who has opened my eyes,
salutations unto thee, O gracious guru!

* * *

The majlis sat in complete silence. Everyone was filled with a sense of wonder. Vini looked at the sky as tears rolled down his cheeks. Pink and orange wisps of cirrus clouds seemed to burn a beautiful pattern on the still blue sky as dusk fell. The sky turned bright amber for a few moments. It was the *godhuli vela*, the most entrancing moment of the evening, when dust raised by the cows coming home creates a surreal and transcendental atmosphere.

12

Hell's Gate

Jay's brain was quite foggy when Pam's driver dropped him off at Defence Colony. The driver offered to help him as he almost fell out of the car, but Jay refused and waved him off. It was dark except for the faint yellow light from the streetlamp.

He fumbled with the gate and pushed it open. The metal gate squeaked loudly, and Jay cursed under his breath. He stumbled and pushed the loudly protesting gate to close it and turned towards the house. He immediately stepped into the familiar puddle of water and cursed as he nearly slipped. Then the bright porch light came on, almost blinding him.

Jay staggered up the two steps to the porch. The metal grill door was locked from inside as always. He began fumbling for the bell when he realized that Satish was standing inside and watching him quietly, with his arms folded across his chest.

'Are you drunk, Jay?'

Jay didn't reply as he tried to push his hand through the grill to open the latch.

'It's locked,' Satish said grimly. Hearing the clattering, Shubhra had come out. She reached out for the key to the door. 'No, Shubhra. I am not letting a drunkard into our house.' Satish said without removing his gaze from Jay. Shubhra looked extremely conflicted and helpless.

'Open the door, Ma.' Jay was slowly registering the fact that this was intentional.

Satish shook his head slowly. 'No.'

Shubhra tried to plead with her husband through her rapidly brimming eyes. Her lips trembled, but no words formed. 'Enough is enough, Shubhra. We have talked about this. Jay has embarrassed us enough.'

'What's your problem, Dad? This is my house too. Open this goddamn door!' Jay was shaking in anger. His knuckles had turned white as he gripped the grill hard.

'Son, what you do with your life is none of my business. But what you are doing nowadays is not what we have taught you. You have become a despicable person, Jay. You insulted all your classmates in public and fought with Raghav. Yes, Jay, I know everything. And not from Raghav. Word gets around, you know. You have been continuously bribing people to get projects. Many of your clients are criminals under investigation. You forget, I was in the government too. They respected me for my honesty, Jay. And now, you have done everything to shame us. We cannot show our face anywhere without people mentioning your antics!'

Both father and son had huge egos, and they lashed out at each other. Suddenly, all the old rancour and bitterness pent up inside Jay exploded. 'Dad! You have been a pathetic and useless pushover! You have done nothing in your life except push files! Even this house belongs to your father. You couldn't make anything at all! Why do you keep showing off your stupid honesty to the world? What did it get you? You didn't even make it to undersecretary! And what about Ma? You treat her like your personal servant! You call yourself an honourable man? *Bullshit*! First learn to be a good husband!'

'JAY! HOW DARE YOU!' Satish was livid. Shubhra was desperately trying to get between them, and this angered him further. He pushed her out of his line of sight. 'You stay out of this, Shubhra!'

Shubhra nearly lost her balance, and Jay screamed, 'Maaa!' He shook the grill gate angrily. 'Don't you touch her, you brute! You call yourself a man, come out and fight me! Bloody good-for-nothing! I am ashamed to call you dad.'

Jay looked at his mother. He was shouting now. 'Ma! Come with me right now. Leave this ungrateful man and come as you are! I will make you live like a queen, not like this fellow's servant! Ma please come with me!'

Shubhra spoke haltingly, 'Jay, béta, please calm down. Neighbours can hear you. Please, béta!'

'Let them hear, Ma. Everyone should know about this guy! I know he has never hurt you physically, but he doesn't love you! He orders you around. Why do you listen to him? Come with me, Ma!'

'Jay, please. *Chup ho ja béta*!' Shubhra was sobbing.

'Get out of my house right now!' Satish hissed at Jay. 'And don't show your face to me, ever! GET OUT NOW!'

'Ma, come with me, right now. Leave this guy. Only then will he understand your worth!' Jay was pleading now.

'Get out or I will call the police!' Satish growled. He hadn't moved from his position all through the altercation. 'Shubhra, you want to go, go with him. I leave it to you.' Saying this, Satish turned and marched inside. He sat down on his favourite sofa and buried his face inside the day's newspaper.

Shubhra stood stock-still. Tears were streaming down her cheeks.

'Ma, please come with me?' It sounded more like a question. Jay was pleading again.

Shubhra slowly turned and went inside as Jay kept calling out to her. His voice gradually lost its edge, and he stood there whispering for Shubhra to come with him. Shubhra stood at the locked door and wept, but she didn't come outside.

Almost half an hour later, the metal gate squeaked open, and then, it was shut very slowly as Jay closed the door on his parents, and they on their only son.

The porch light went out.

* * *

As he walked away, Jay cried. Even in his addled state, he realized that he didn't have any family or friends. No one seemed to understand him at all. He felt totally unloved and alone as he left his home behind and took a long walk into the night.

He soon got tired and sat down under a flyover, resting against a pillar. He saw a beggar family with four children, including an infant, squatting some distance away. The woman was cooking something on firewood. There was an altercation going on between the man and the woman, and soon, the infant began crying. As Jay watched, the mother breastfed the baby while stirring the gruel, and she continued shouting at the man, who also kept grumbling. Jay couldn't recall when he had drifted into fitful sleep.

The train is entering a tunnel as he is running behind it, flapping his arms. The suitcases have opened, and all the stuff is spilling out.

'Stop! Stop! Please wait for me! I have to get on this train. Please stop!'

Ritika is laughing shrilly as she flies upside down above him, sitting in his Mercedes, and zooms into the train . . .

'Bye bye! Hahahaha!'

Clothes, papers, books, CDs . . . all his memories fly around like feathers, and his whole life begins tumbling out . . .

Everything is floating around in slow motion as he tries to grab things and put them back into the suitcases . . . but it seems nothing wants to stay inside the suitcases. Things keep floating out as soon as he stuffs them in . . .

He has to hurry; the train is going to disappear . . .

The tunnel is so close now . . . he is ready to enter the last bogie . . . it is just beyond his reach . . . one more inch and he will be able to catch the railing . . .

Suddenly, he sees Shyam and Girish standing between him and the train. As he reaches close to the railing, they stretch out and hold each other's hands, right between him and the railing of the last bogie, blocking his way.

'First give us our money . . . give us your gold, give us your silver . . .'

As he tries to push them away, Shubhra calls him from behind . . .

'Jayyyy . . .' *she grabs at his shirt and wails piteously.*

He now hears a booming voice above himself and looks up to see a giant Satish looming over him. Satish is shaking his index finger and pointing away from the train.

'Get out . . .' Satish roars. His voice echoes from all around and becomes a chorus of voices as hundreds of forms of Satish appear everywhere around Jay.

The train is hooting and clanging incessantly.

Hundreds of Satish voices start roaring,

'G E T O U T O F M Y H O U S E!

R I G H T N O WWWW!'

'You are in dangerrrrr . . . Don't get on the train bétaaaa . . .' *he hears Shubhra's cries through the echoing voices of Satish and the hooting of the train . . .*

The train has nearly disappeared into the tunnel and its horn continues blaring. The couplings clang over the rails, echoing through the tunnel . . .

Whooooooo . . . hooo-hooooooo . . .
Clang clang clang . . .
Mmmooooooooo . . . Mmmooooooo . . .
Mmmooooooo . . .
Dinngg, dinngg, dinngg . . .

Jay awoke with a start to the sound from a nearby loudspeaker.

Day was breaking to the sounds of a conch shell and bells, mixed with mantra chants from some temple close by. Soon, the strains of a shabad and the soulful azaan, from a gurdwara and a mosque nearby, were creating a unique symphony. He kept his eyes shut, soaking in the magical atmosphere.

When he opened his eyes, he discovered that there was a stray dog sleeping next to him. It got up with a start and began wagging its tail. Jay patted it as he looked up and saw the beggar family huddled together, sleeping peacefully. The man and woman must have made up, as they were sleeping facing each other, and the woman's arm was on the man's shoulder.

Jay stood up slowly, dusting himself. He was feeling pretty dreadful. His mouth felt acidic and dry, his head was throbbing and his body was protesting painfully. He seemed to have pulled a back muscle, and his bladder felt as if it would burst. He looked around and saw a darkened corner a few yards away. He walked there quickly, and the strong smell told him that the place was already being used as a urinating point. Not seeing anyone, he relieved himself quickly, and rushed out, feeling like a petty thief.

Jay stretched himself to get rid of his stiffness and began walking stiffly on the road once again. The sun had risen, and the city was beginning to come to life.

Jay got on the road adjacent to the flyover. He followed the sounds of a bhajan playing, possibly at the same temple whose conch-shell sounds had woken him up. He passed a throng of devotees, with bright vermillion *tikas*, coming out of a temple right next to the road. A little ahead, he noticed men wearing white skullcaps emerging from a mosque. As he left the flyover behind, Jay could see the golden spires of the gurdwara on the other side of the flyover. The shabad was still on. Everyone around him looked happy and peaceful.

Somehow, before Jay realized it, his feet were taking him towards Raghav's home. He stopped mid-stride and became pensive. He was really missing the only true friend he had ever had.

An autorickshaw passed him and stopped a little ahead. The Sikh driver, having seen Jay bent over and walking slowly, asked him if he needed a ride. He must have come out of the gurdwara just now, Jay guessed. Jay said he didn't have money on him. The driver said he could Paytm the fare to him. Jay shrugged, shook his head and decided to go to Raghav's place in the autorickshaw.

They reached the gate to Raghav's colony just as Arushi's school bus arrived. Jay asked the driver to stop some distance away from the bus stand. Jay didn't get down. Sitting in the autorickshaw, he watched his estranged friend wistfully.

Raghav was standing with Arushi. The girl was chatting away happily with her father, who kept nodding seriously as he guided her towards the bus. He helped Arushi, as well as a couple of other children, on to the bus. He waved to her as the bus left and turned to head back to his home.

Jay watched Raghav return to the colony. He continued to stare at the gate for a few minutes until the driver broke his reverie, asking Jay if he was going to get off. Jay shook his head pensively before asking the surprised driver to take him to Hauz Khas.

13

The Singer on the Beach

'Have you found the ultimate truth?' asked a family man who had been coming to the majlis to listen to Vini since the beginning.

Vini spoke softly, 'Who is the knower of this world? Is it me? Who is this seeker of the truth? Is it "I"? What is this "I"? Where do I search for my real self? I have been wandering through existence for aeons.'

'Talk to us about awakening, O master.'

'Do I even remember when I started on this path? The beginning is lost in the mists of time. Was there "time" then? I have been born ten thousand times. I have died ten thousand times. I have journeyed for so long through eternity. I have now turned back to go home.

'I can now see far into the fathomless abyss of time—listening to the celestial fugue while I dance forever with my infinite selves. I have travelled through many, many lands and have lived and died in many, many worlds. I have ventured into ten thousand bodies.

With mothers and fathers, sisters and brothers, wives and children.

'And yet, this journey has just begun. Many more adventures await me, I am sure. I have many more worlds to wander through. The stars and galaxies are my playmates, the cosmos is my playground. I have begun my journey back to where I came from. I am homeward-bound.'

The majlis sat spellbound. Vini's words spoke of mysteries that they did not understand. And yet, what he said intrigued the rare few who had tasted the nectar of meditation.

Vini continued Ash's tale, 'Ashwini felt an exquisite joy when Ajaat gave him his new name. He danced in the forest as he sang of Tuka's inexpressible joy of awakening.'

Vini burst into song spontaneously,

'Aanandaachey Dohii aanandataranga
aanandachi anga aanandaachey.
Kaay saango dzhaaley kaanhiichiyaa baahi
pudhey tchaali naahi aawadiiney.
Garbhaachey aawadi maatechaa dohalaa
tethinchaa jiwhaalaa tethey bimbey.
Tukaa mhaney, taisaa otalaasey t'thasaa
anubhava sarisaa mukhaa aalaa,'

'Frissons of delight arise
in this deep pool of exquisite bliss!
This entire body of bliss is ecstatic joy itself!
How can I say what happened?
It's something incomprehensible

and inexpressible in words!
No worldly path charms me
to move ahead on it any more!
That which is craved deep within the womb,
is desired by the mother.
Rapture for that inner being
manifests itself as a glowing halo.
Tuka says that his lips have spoken true words
of this absolutely real experience,
which appeared like a river in his mouth . . .'

The magical moment felt eternal as it hung suspended in time . . . Vini broke the spell as he continued his own story.

* * *

It had now been over twelve years since Ash had joined Ajaat. Many teachers and an administrator had joined the school. Some young men had started other service projects under Ash's guidance. Ajaat told Ash to appoint senior teachers to take his legacy forward within the tribal region. Ash ensured that Ajaat's work would continue through a trust. In keeping with Ajaat's wish, Ash declined to be on its board.

Ajaat was now completely blind and could only hear faintly from one ear. He was extremely frail and lay on his cot nearly all day. He refused medication saying his life would take its own course, as a river merging into the ocean. Ash insisted on personally taking care of Ajaat, despite there being a number of young men and women to serve the master. He would wash him tenderly and clean his excretions with love. He fed his master with his own hands and sat at his feet holding his hand. He propped Ajaat up so that he wouldn't choke on his own saliva, and constantly turned his listless body so that he wouldn't get sores. Ajaat's eyes watered, and he cried watching Ash taking care of him. Ash saw this as his seva to his guru and felt immense joy at serving Ajaat. He hardly ever left Ajaat's side, except to conduct satsang or for extremely important work of the school, and rushed back as quickly as he could.

Soon, the day arrived when Ajaat's breathing became laboured, and he called for Ash repeatedly. Ash was at a satsang and rushed back to the hut. He sent everyone away as he sat at his master's side. Ajaat held his hand tightly as he struggled to speak.

'Vini béta, my time has arrived. Now, you must spread the knowledge to the world. You will not be able to do it here, in this forest. You must leave for the city that you knew long ago. Teach those people who can bring joy to the world. Don't waste any time with crowds. Choose the ones who can bring change in society. Teach them to be good human beings. Teach them through your songs, béta.'

'*Aamaar jaabaar shomoy holo, dao bidaay.*
Mochho aankhi duaar kholo, dao bidaay.'

'The time has come for me to leave, do say goodbye.
Wipe your tears, open the door and bid farewell.'

Ash wept as he held his master's hand. He knew the final moments were nigh. Ajaat asked Ash to bring him his ektara. He could barely hold it. He said, 'This is yours from today, my dearest béta. Go and sing songs of joy to heal the people. Go and spread wisdom in the world. Leave this place as soon as I am gone, my dearest Vini béta.

> 'Ja. Andheron mein thokar khaye huon
> ka chirag ban.'

'Go. Be a lamp
unto ones who are stumbling in the dark.'

Ash held the ektara to his bosom as he sobbed softly. Ajaat used his last ounce of breath and whispered, 'Sing to me, béta.'

> 'Aaguner parashmani chhnoaao praaney,
> e jibon punnyo karo dohon daaney.
> Aamar ei dehokhaani tuley dharo,
> tomaar oi debaaloyer prodip karo.
> Nishidin aalok-shikhaa jwoluk gaaney,
> Aandharer gaaye gaaye parash tabo,
> saara raat photaak taara nabo nabo.
> Nayoner drishti hotey ghuchbey kaalo,
> jekhaney porbe sethaay dekhbey aalo.
> Byatha mor utthbey jwoley urdho-paaney.'

'Caress my soul with the fiery touchstone,
purify this existence by setting me ablaze.

Hold aloft this mortal body in flames,
make it illumine thy holy refuge.
Allow this spire of blazing light
to burn night and day with holy chants!
When darkness would be touched
by this fire again and again,
Many many new stars will be born
and spontaneously begin to light up.
These eyes will then find
nary a spot of blackness at all,
there shall be light anywhere one glances!
And then, all my pain and suffering
would be consigned to the flames,
rising high into the lofty firmament . . .'

Ajaat put his trembling hand on Ash's head as he finally collapsed. He left his body soon afterwards, just after midnight. Ash wept inconsolably as he sang Ajaat's favourite songs plucking at his ektara until blood oozed from his finger. Others came in quietly and stood weeping—they too joined in with Ash and sang.

Hours passed. Ajaat's body had to be prepared for the funeral. Word had spread, and the local villagers from all around started congregating around the hillock. Ash refused to leave the side of the departed master. He did not stop singing to his master. As day broke, the other devotees had to gently help him get up.

As the sun rose, Ajaat's body was placed for the final darshan, for all his devotees to pay their last respects, in the school's courtyard. The great soul was finally consecrated to the flames that afternoon itself, with Ash doing the rituals. Thousands thronged to have the final glimpse of their gracious and simple teacher. Ash sat next to the burning pyre all night, unmoving. As dawn arrived, he touched the ashes with reverence. The embers were still warm.

Soon thereafter, Ash completed the final rituals of consecrating Ajaat's *asthiyaan*, his mortal remains, into a stream close to Ajaat's hut, and prepared to leave the forest forever. The other disciples wanted Ash to remain at the school and take Ajaat's place, but he refused, as he had been instructed by Ajaat. He promised to visit them whenever he could.

Ash left the forest that afternoon. Many of Ajaat's devotees and the hundreds of villagers who had come to pay their last respects to Ajaat followed him out, to bid him farewell.

Ash arrived at the beedi shop and met Mangal's youngest son, who ran the shop now. He told the young man that he was leaving for good. The boy tearfully asked Ash to conduct one last satsang for the villagers. Ash agreed and sang to the villagers.

Before he left the land of his awakening forever, on the instructions of his master, Ash sat down at the tea stall and drank the sweet tea one last time. He then proceeded to the nearest bus stop, followed by the entire village, his schoolteachers and hundreds of school students.

* * *

In his forty-eighth year, Ash reached his home city once again. He began calling himself Vini, the name given to him by his master. He had an important task to fulfil, as desired by Ajaat. He was now on a sincere search for deserving students who had the capacity to transform society.

No one remembered Ashwini Kumar Singh any more. Sixteen years had passed since the dying man had cursed him at his birthday party. Vini often wondered whether that was really a curse or a boon. When his entire world had come crashing down, he hadn't a clue that the calamity would lead him to Ajaat and on his journey of awakening.

Today, he was in a completely different state of mind. His health was better than when he had left the city years ago. He had absolutely no idea where his wife and daughters were, and he wished them well. The city had completely changed too. Vini couldn't recognize most of the places he had known when he lived there. But he was on a mission now, and nothing else mattered.

Vini chose to spend his days at the beaches around the city. The sea reminded him of his master Ajaat. Every day, he would come to the beach and sing. Soon, people began calling him 'the singing storyteller' on the beach. Gradually, a few people started going up to him to listen to his songs. Some thought that he was a beggar and dropped money in front of him. Others saw him as a *fakir*, a wandering minstrel, and bowed to him. Vini saw them all as humans on a journey to reach happiness. He mostly sang *nirgun* poetry with his master's ektara.

'Kar na fakiri phir kyaa dilgiiri,
sadaa magan mein rehnaa ji.
Koi din gaadi na, koi din banglaa,
koi din jangal basnaa ji.
Koi din haathi na, koi din ghodaa,
koi din paidal chalnaa ji.
Koi din khaaja na, koi din laado,
koi din phaakam phaakaa ji.
Koi din d'huliyaa, koi din talaa'i,
koi din bhuin par lautnaa ji.
Meera kahe prabhu girdhar naagar,
aay padey so sehenaa ji.'

A few foreign tourists began visiting him at the beach, and one of them asked another what the man was singing about. As they struggled to piece the words together, Vini smiled and stopped singing. He then explained the song in fluent English, to the surprised tourists:

'Once you become a liberated pauper,
what worldly enjoyments would you want,
always remaining immersed in the self?
Someday in a carriage, someday in a mansion
and someday as a forest-dweller!
Someday riding on a royal elephant,
someday on a warrior's horse
and someday plodding along on foot!
Someday eating fried khaja pastries,
someday having sweet laddoos
and someday nothing at all!
Someday the pomp of drums,

someday eking a living as a labourer
and someday going back into the ground!
Meerabai proclaims, by the grace of her lord,
the great mountain-holder,
one has to bear whatever befalls one's lot.'

The foreigners were mesmerized. They hadn't expected this singing fakir to be such an eloquent speaker. They called out to their large group of friends who were scattered on the beach. Everyone came and sat around Vini as he regaled them with many songs, followed by beautiful translations. Vini's explanations were much admired by the listeners.

From that day onwards, it became Vini's practice to share the meanings of his songs after he sang. This unique style made a huge impact on the younger listeners and the foreign tourists.

One day, a group of young people, who were part of a nationwide campaign to clean the beaches and raise social awareness, asked him to sing for their cause at sunset. They all gathered around him after clearing the beach of dirt and garbage. Vini acquiesced happily. The youth loved his performance and invited him to their college to perform. The evening was a hit with the students, and Vini was invited to a few other colleges.

Soon, he was featured as 'the singer on the beach' in an international documentary. Numerous articles followed. Vini became popular on social media and television, and began getting invitations to conferences and seminars on mystic music.

He never revealed his true identity to anyone, until eight years later at the airport lounge, when a man named Jay, through a stroke of luck, recognized who he was.

* * *

Vini smiled softly as he concluded his tale. The majlis had lived through his life with him. They had laughed and cried with him. And now that the fascinating tale had reached its end, there were tears in many eyes. People came up to touch Vini's feet and take his blessings. His old friends hugged him. Everyone wanted him to share more wisdom with them. Vini assured the majlis that he would come and address them occasionally.

'Viniji, we wanted to ask you something,' Suketu, the young software engineer, said once everyone had dispersed. 'We have talked to an FM radio channel about you, and they are keen to host you at live events in different public venues on Friday afternoons. Would you be able to come?'

'Of course, Suketu. I would love to,' Vini said, smiling. 'Maybe there is someone that the universe wants me to sing for. I am just the medium. Maybe someone's life will be transformed through divine grace.'

14

The Dark Night

It was almost 8 a.m. when Jay reached Ritika's apartment. She was irritable in the mornings and took a long time to open the door. When she saw Jay she snapped at him, 'Where have you been, Jay? I was so worried! And look at you. Did you fall into a garbage bin or something? Please get cleaned up. And, don't touch anything with your grubby hands!'

Jay didn't say anything to her. He looked defeated as he went inside. Ritika was a bit surprised that he didn't retaliate. She sensed that there was something wrong, but she didn't pursue it. She didn't really care about Jay's well-being anyway. Sahil had asked her to join him on a trip to Mauritius, and she had to go through a few more weeks with Jay. She nimbly ran up to her bedroom and crashed immediately. Jay slowly followed her up the stairs and went in for a shower. He left for work in less than an hour without eating anything. This time he didn't forget his keys to the apartment. He had already messaged and called the other partners for an emergency meeting at noon.

As soon as Shyam, Girish and Pam joined him, he stood up and declared quietly, 'I am not going to take on any of the projects where we need to pay a bribe. ALSOL has only two projects going on right now, and once these are over, I will only work on clean and above-board projects that we get strictly on merit. I will not take any of the profits until I return all the money to each of you.'

'What are you talking about Jay?' Girish said, looking surprised. 'You only said that we cannot do anything without paying money under the table! What's happened to you?'

Shyam was frowning. He didn't say a word.

Pam spoke slowly, 'Jay, what's going on? Is it about yesterday? We can discuss all projects one by one before we take a call.'

'It's not open to discussion, Pam. I created ALSOL. I cannot see it degenerate into a money-churning enterprise.'

'Then it is better *you* leave, Jay,' Shyam spoke for the first time. 'And, since we are at a loss because of your individual decisions, you can pay us our money. Then you can do whatever you feel like.'

'Shyam, you very well know I don't have the money to pay you all. We are partners, and all payments were a collective decision,' Jay retorted.

'Exactly, Jay. Everything has been decided collectively so far, and will be so in the future. Even today's decision. ALSOL cannot run by your rules alone. Our first priority is recovering our ten crore. By any means whatsoever,' Shyam spoke in a measured tone.

Jay shook his head. He wasn't ready to change his mind now. 'Do whatever you wish. I will not change my mind.' He walked out quickly, without looking back.

With Jay's decision to go the honest way, ALSOL began to lose business rapidly.

As predicted by Jay's dad, it was Shyam who ensured that Jay was completely ruined. Pam was coerced to side with them by her husband, Arjun, whose money she had given Jay. A couple of days later, Shyam, in consultation with lawyers, called for a vote for removing Jay from ALSOL. Girish agreed immediately. Jay was shocked when he was thrown out of the very company that he had created, for incompetently running the enterprise. To Jay's surprise, Pam had also voted against him, citing her husband's disinclination to support Jay.

Jay was forced to sign off ALSOL to Shyam, Girish and Pam. Shyam made sure Jay didn't get a single rupee. Jay was informed that, on the contrary, it was he who would now have to pay ALSOL the huge sum of Rs 65 lakh, or he would be arrested for embezzlement and non-payment of company dues. ALSOL's assets were worth about Rs 8 crore, and Jay had withdrawn nearly three crore over the years. Shyam and Girish made certain that the company account books now showed that all the cheques encashed by Jay for various bribes were, in fact, for his personal use.

Except the two ongoing projects, every other project that Jay had brought to ALSOL fell through, despite Shyam and Girish trying to run the company.

Pam hardly ever came to the office or the meetings any more, citing the studies of her children.

Jay's Mercedes was seized by Shyam for ALSOL, to recover dues for the company. Jay asked Ritika to help him out by selling a couple of diamonds and gold jewellery that he'd gifted her. Ritika hemmed and hawed, saying the stuff was kept in a bank locker. Three days later, Jay woke up in the morning and found that Ritika had disappeared.

Jay sadly realized that he had been giving Ritika whatever she had wanted, and the moment he needed something from her, she had shown her true colours. He finally understood what his parents and friends had been telling him all along, that she had no interest in his well-being and was only looking out for her own comforts. He blocked the credit card he had given her. She had continued to use it after leaving him, and the bill ran into lakhs.

Pam came to meet Jay, who was not keen to see her. She had betrayed his trust. Pam tried to explain that it wasn't her fault, but to no avail. She said that she had voted against Jay on the insistence of Arjun, as he had put in her share of the money. Jay just shook his head and showed her the door. She felt guilty and helpless, and offered to help Jay get out of the mess. Jay refused point-blank, asking her to leave immediately. He requested her not to visit him ever again. Pam kept saying sorry and wept as she left.

The flat owner sent Jay a notice to vacate the apartment in a month's time, as the rent hadn't been paid for over two months.

Jay was in debt of nearly Rs 40 lakh. His father eventually bailed him out by selling his blue-chip shares. Jay came to know that his dad had met Shyam, Pam and Girish, and offered to pay off Jay's dues. In exchange, all charges against Jay were to be dropped and ALSOL was to be dissolved. Shyam and Girish agreed immediately. Pam refused to take her share.

* * *

'Where are you, Jayyy? Jay, where are youuuu?'

'Here! I am here, Maaaa!'

Jay is groping in the darkness. It feels thick and heavy. Almost like tar.

He can't see his ma, and he stumbles and falls down. He is clawing at the blackness as it begins to take the shape of a huge palm that grips his throat, not letting him breathe. He begins gasping as he cries out for his mother.

Then, he hears his dad calling him, 'Jay bétaaa, where are you?'

Jay cries out, 'Daaaad! I am here. Please help me, Dad! I don't want to die.'

Suddenly, a young, twelve-year-old Raghav's face appears in front of him, bright and shining. 'Jay! I am going to play cricket!' Raghav runs past him happily.

'Hahaha . . . We are going to play. We are going to winnnnn!'

'Rags, take me with you! I want to play. Please don't go, Rags! Don't leave me. Pleeeease . . .'

Jay begins to get up, and then he hears a rumbling.
As he stands up, the train rushes right at him and hoots
loudly, as it hits him . . .
Whooooo . . . whooooo-whooooo . . .
CRASHHHH!
Aaahhh . . .

Jay had twitched and jerked in his sleep, and he had
fallen off the bed, hitting his head on the floor. He
groaned and lay there, listless . . .

Jay gradually began to fall into depression. He did
not want to meet anybody. He soon left the Hauz Khas
apartment without telling anyone where he was going.
He had found a small one-room tenement close to a mall
at the other end of the city, far from everyone he knew.

The room rent was next to nothing. It was rundown
and dingy, but Jay hardly noticed all that. In fact, he
hardly noticed anything nowadays. It was as if a dark
blackness had begun to envelop him. His mind was
numb, and he remained uninterested in most things.

As he was unpacking his things at the new place, he
came across a couple of books and some old photographs
from his IIM days that he must have brought over from
his home when he had shifted to Hauz Khas. In one of
the fading pictures, he was standing in front of a wall
inside his IIM room. Behind him, painted in large red
letters on the wall, was a quote,

'With indomitable will,
you can reach anywhere you want.'

—Ashwini Kumar Singh

Ashwini Kumar Singh.

A vision of an ektara string snapping flashed in front of his eyes.

Vini.

He clearly remembered Vini. That meeting was etched in his mind. He felt slightly energized and tried to search for Vini on the Internet but could not find him. He immediately felt deflated and hopeless, and dropped the idea. This had become a regular thing with him. He would give up at the first sign of discomfort and failure. He didn't seem to find anything worth pushing himself for. He felt a vacuum inside.

* * *

Three months had passed since Jay had had the bitter fight with his father. Shubhra and Satish were devastated after Jay's departure. He wasn't taking Shubhra's phone calls, but she could see the 'last seen' on WhatsApp and deduced that he did come online intermittently. Shubhra had even gone and met Raghav, who had politely refused to get involved.

Satish hardly spoke nowadays. He was completely broken from inside. His son hadn't ever understood his constraints. Satish had spent most of his savings in getting his father's younger brother to withdraw a court case that the uncle had lodged against Satish's father, claiming their house. It was absurd, as the land had been allocated to Satish's father because he was a soldier. However, Satish had paid the uncle a huge lump sum at the behest of his father, who was quite unwell at the time. Once he got the uncle off his father's back, expenses mounted further in taking care of his father since he'd had a heart attack and then, a stroke. All this had happened when Jay was an infant. But the greatest drain on Satish's finances had been in the care of Jay's elder sister, who had cerebral palsy and had died at the age of fifteen, before Jay had turned three.

Predictably, Satish and Shubhra had been extremely protective of Jay as he grew up. They never saved anything, and got him the best possible education and facilities. Sadly, Jay had been thoroughly spoiled, and the result was right in front of them.

* * *

Jay didn't realize it, but he was wading into the deep waters of depression. The darkness was engulfing him slowly but surely. He would sit in the room locked up, and he kept his phone switched off. Once in a while, when he opened it, there were hundreds of unread messages, which he deleted without even looking at them.

Jay's depression wrapped its claws around him, and he started withdrawing into a shell. He had not been eating well for months now, and he had lost a lot of weight.

Gradually, Jay began to feel utterly hopeless. He didn't want to talk to anyone. He didn't make eye contact with anyone. He wouldn't bathe or eat for days, and hardly spoke a word with anyone. He just sat next to a window and looked outside, staring at nothing in particular. His dreams were becoming more and more bizarre.

A month passed. He decided there was no hope of redemption and began entertaining thoughts of ending it all . . .

* * *

As winter set in, he began to feel lower and lower, and one early afternoon, he woke up gloomily and saw that he had almost no money. Whatever cash he had was just enough for one cup of his favourite cappuccino at the mall. Jay got to the mall and bought rat poison, which looked like a green-coloured chocolate bar. Then, he went into a coffee shop and bought his favourite cappuccino in a styrofoam cup with a lid. He sat down quietly at an empty table and began scrolling through his phone, looking at pictures of his dad and mom with him, as he sipped his last coffee.

All of a sudden, he heard an announcement and people clapping. Then, he heard a man singing.

'Bulleya! Ki jaana main kaun!'

Jay got up slowly. The voice was hauntingly familiar. He picked up the coffee cup and began walking towards the sound slowly.

'Na main momin vich maseetaan,
Na main vich kufar diyan reetaan . . .'

Through the corridor, he reached the atrium. He was on the third level, saw a banner and guessed this was a promotional programme organized by the city's popular FM radio station.

'*Na main paakaan vich paleetaan,*
Na main moosa na firown!'

He spotted a man with an ektara, singing on a small stage.

'*Bulleya ki jaana main kaun!*'

Suddenly, Jay realized it was Vini. 'Ashwini Sir! V-Vini Sir!' He began running towards the singer excitedly. He was stopped by the security guards. 'Please let me go. I need to meet him!' He sounded desperate.

The song ended and the crowd thronged Vini. Jay pushed himself through the melee, but he found that the stage was empty. Jay inquired for Vini desperately, but the mall security head told Jay that Vini had left immediately after the concert, and they had no clue where to find him, since the organizers had left with him.

Disappointed, Jay began walking away. The cappuccino had become lukewarm, and he decided to sit down on a bench near the stage and finish it.

Moments later, he heard a familiar voice behind him, asking if he could join him.

'Vini!' Jay's face lit up as he turned and saw Vini smiling compassionately.

'Absolutely right. In the flesh!' Vini laughed. They hugged and sat down.

Jay suddenly felt something come alive inside him. It was the first spark of happiness he had felt in months.

15

The Karmic ATM

'I confess, it took me a while to place you, Jay. I was almost at the exit by the time I remembered. You look so different!' Vini exclaimed. 'It's been, what . . . around six months, since we met at the airport?'

'Just over eight months, actually,' Jay replied.

'Ah! Yes. I was going to Prague for the seminar on mystic music. I will be going again this year. This time, it is going to be held in San Francisco.' Jay nodded, lips pursed, as he tried to keep his emotions in check.

Vini had his ektara in a black bag, which resembled a narrow violin case, slung over his shoulder. 'It's such a pleasant surprise to meet you once again, Jay. I clearly remember our early-morning encounter and conversation at the airport lounge. To be honest, I did wonder on occasion what had happened to you.'

'A lot has happened during these months, Vini. I really wish I hadn't forgotten to take your number that morning,' Jay mumbled.

'Things come to pass, when they are meant to, Jay,' Vini said softly.

Jay nodded slowly. Vini could see that Jay was in terrible shape. He appeared unkempt. His clothes were faded and frayed. There were dark circles around his eyes, and he appeared to have lost a lot of weight.

'You look very tired, Jay,' Vini said. His voice was filled with concern.

Jay nodded, avoiding his stare. He looked down at the rapidly blurring logo design on the coffee cup as tears welled up in his eyes. The muscles of his jaw ached as he clenched and unclenched them. He realized that he couldn't hold his emotions back any longer. He covered his face with his palms and began sobbing softly.

'Oh, Jay,' Vini almost whispered. 'Why have you done this to yourself?' Jay felt Vini's hand on his head, tousling his hair. He looked up slowly, through his tears. His world was a blur.

Vini was looking at him. His eyes were filled with compassion. There was a hint of a gentle smile playing on his lips. He patted Jay on his cheek lightly before pulling his hand back. 'You look like you haven't been sleeping well. Do you have a place to sleep?'

'I have a small room close by,' Jay said softly.

'When did you last have a proper meal?' Vini was frowning slightly. He knew the young man's answer even before Jay mumbled, 'Not in a very long time.'

'Hmm . . . Get up. Let's go and have a hot meal together, and then we shall talk.'

Jay had tears rolling down his cheeks as he stood up. He looked completely defeated. 'I can't, Vini . . . I shouldn't,' he stammered. 'You hardly know me.'

Vini stood up quickly. He had the energy of a man a third his age. He patted Jay on his shoulder. 'Of course, I know you. You are Jay, my early-morning-airport-lounge friend.' He held his ektara in one hand and kept the other one on Jay's back, gently pushing him along.

They entered a quiet restaurant and sat down at a secluded table tucked in a corner. Jay kept silent as Vini quickly summoned a waiter and ordered a salad, aloo–pudina raita, savoury matar paneer, an aromatic yellow dal seasoned with ghee, jeera rice and tandoori rotis. He also called for some lightly spiced buttermilk, or masala chaas, to be served immediately.

Vini watched Jay as he gulped down the cold chaas. Almost immediately, Jay began to feel rejuvenated. Soon food arrived, and Vini insisted that they both eat before talking. Jay ate quickly and Vini, as usual, ate frugally and at an unhurried pace. Watching him, Jay also tried to slow down but found it difficult. Once his meal was over, Jay waited for Vini to finish. It seemed like an eternity to him before Vini finished his spartan lunch. He seemed to be enjoying each morsel, closing his eyes and deliberately chewing and savouring it for a long time before taking his next bite.

Vini smiled, took a deep breath and said, 'Well, Jay, I can see that your string's nearly snapped. We really need to do something about that very quickly.'

Jay nodded silently, looking down. Hesitatingly, he shared all that he had been through over the past eight months.

Vini said, 'You have really gone through a lot, Jay. But why have you lost hope? You are made of much sterner stuff.'

'I can't see a way forward, Vini. My partners nearly sent me to jail, my girlfriend walked out on me, my only real friend doesn't wish to have anything to do with me, and my parents refuse to let me into my . . . their home. My father had to bail me out of a debt of lakhs, but he refuses to even look at me. I have tried to *let things be*, as you had said when we met at the airport, but it's landed me in worse trouble.'

Vini nodded slowly. After a long pause, he said, 'There's a well-known story of an old farmer and his horse. You might have heard it, but let me share it with you . . .'

* * *

An old farmer had a young son. They owned a white horse. One day, the horse ran away. The farmer's neighbours said, 'This is really unfortunate.'

'Maybe that is so,' the farmer replied. 'And then, maybe not!'

A couple of days later, the horse came back. With it were three more wild horses! The neighbours came to the farmer and said excitedly, 'You are really so fortunate!'

'Maybe that is so,' the farmer replied. 'And then, maybe not!'

Days passed. The farmer's young son decided to train the wild horses and mounted one of them. The wild horse bolted, throwing the boy off, and he broke his leg. The neighbours were sympathetic. 'Your son has been crippled. This is truly unfortunate!'

'Maybe that is so,' the farmer replied. 'And then, maybe not!'

Time passed. A few months later, the kingdom was attacked by enemies. The army lost many soldiers. The emperor declared that all able-bodied men of the kingdom were to be drafted into the army and sent to fight.

Since the farmer's son had a bad leg, he was excused. The neighbours came and told the farmer, 'All our sons are facing danger on the battlefield. Your son is with you. You are so fortunate!'

'Maybe that is so,' the farmer replied. 'And then, maybe not!'

And so, life went on, filled with ups and downs.

* * *

'It's a very nice story, Vini. But, how is it relevant to me?' asked Jay.

Vini said, 'Jay, nothing is permanent. What the farmer's neighbours perceived as fortunate or unfortunate, wasn't really so. In our lives, what we might believe to be misfortune could turn out to be something fortunate in a different set of circumstances.'

Jay smiled wistfully. 'I want to believe this, Vini, but I cannot see how my misfortune can turn into something positive. I know that only you can help me. Meeting you today is the best thing that has happened to me in a very long time, Vini.'

Vini took a long breath and said, 'Jay, no one can help us but ourselves. If we divide our life into piles of good and bad events, like clean clothes and dirty laundry, we will never find peace. We need to experience life as a whole and not in compartments.'

'So what must I do now, Vini? Right now everything is in the dirty laundry pile, which needs washing.' Jay grinned sheepishly.

'Have you ever used an ATM to withdraw cash?' Vini asked Jay.

'Of course!'

'What if you don't have money in your bank? Can you withdraw anything then?'

'No. Unless I use a credit card.'

'Ah! Credit. Yes, that's possible. But then, you need to pay it back, and you are charged interest on the withdrawal, is it not?' Vini smiled.

'Absolutely. But that is something everyone knows, and accepts,' Jay replied.

Vini took a deep breath. 'Our life is similar, Jay. To live in this world, we have to perform actions, or karma. As we act, there are effects or ripples of our actions. These effects come back upon us as fruits of our actions. These fruits of actions appear in our lives as new situations. And, we respond to these new situations by performing a fresh set of actions, or karmas. The interesting part is that the fruits of our actions appear automatically as we navigate through our lives. We have control on our actions but no control on the fruit of our actions.'

Jay nodded. 'Yes, Vini, you are right. I remember reading something like this somewhere . . .'

Vini nodded, 'It is what Krishna proclaimed in Bhagavad Gita, Jay.'

'Karmanyeva adhikarastey
maa phaleshu kadachana.'

'One has the right to action, not to the fruit.'

Jay remembered hearing these words many times. This saying was common knowledge in India. But people hardly abide by pithy wisdom.

Vini continued, 'Look around you, Jay. People are eating and drinking here, in this restaurant. But in the end, they'll have to pay their bills. Isn't it?' Jay nodded.

'Now, suppose someone ordered a sumptuous meal, enjoyed every bit of it and the wonderful service that came with it, and then, decided not to pay the bill. What would happen to them?' Vini asked pointedly.

'The person would be detained by the management, and probably made to wash dishes all day to recover the cost of the meal,' Jay said.

'Right. It's the same with our lives, Jay. We have to pay for whatever we enjoy. Everything gets recovered. It's just a matter of time.'

'There are many people who seem to be enjoying a very good life, without having worked a single day for it, Vini,' Jay said wistfully. 'And then, there are some of us who have worked ourselves to the bone, with nothing to show for it, except failure and suffering.'

'Sometimes, we might be enjoying the benefits of some good deeds done earlier,' Vini said. 'It feels unfair, Jay, but everything has a reason.'

Jay was in deep thought now. Vini added, 'There's a downside too, Jay. We suffer because of unsavoury deeds done earlier as well. You could call these "prepaid" karmic benefits. Look at your own life, Jay. You are well educated. It was because your parents gave you the means and the opportunities, isn't it?' Jay nodded.

'You were born able-bodied, with a healthy mind, to financially stable parents. You had no say in the choice of the school you were sent to. All these were "prepaid" benefits you got. But, you scored good marks at school, and used your education to build a good business. That was you using the education you got, or the fruit of your karma, to create something valuable out of it. Doesn't it logically follow that whatever misery you are suffering right now, is also a consequence of some earlier karma, or how you have acted in the past?' Jay stared at Vini as if a hammer had hit him in his chest.

Vini carried on, 'In fact, we can think of our life as a karmic ATM from which we withdraw pleasant and unpleasant experiences. But here, *what you give is what you get*. You don't have a choice. You cannot keep withdrawing pleasant circumstances from your karmic ATM if you have only deposited unpleasant stuff.'

'What if I decide not to do anything at all? If I don't perform any actions, isn't it logical that I won't make any new problems for myself?' Jay asked.

'That's just like pressing a pause button on your life, Jay. You are only going to prolong your suffering. Someday, you'll have to experience the fruit of your past actions, Jay. Suppose a man stole something from a shop. He could hide for years, but once he comes out of hiding, he will have to face the consequences or fruits of his actions. Isn't that so?'

Jay nodded. Vini was correct. 'But how do I fight, Vini? I have tried and tried. Nothing is working. I see failure at every juncture.' Jay's eyes welled up once more.

'Get a grip on yourself, Jay. You will need to face the consequences of your past actions. Whatever you are going through is very unpleasant, but it will surely end. Hiding ourselves and refusing to face unpleasant situations cannot make our problems disappear. Boats are not built to stay in harbours but to sail on stormy seas.'

'I am ready to face anything, Vini, but I need your guidance,' Jay pleaded.

Vini smiled compassionately. Jay was clawing back. He wanted to fight. He wanted to win. That was a good sign.

'Of course, Jay. You will surely find a way. Providence has brought us together once again, and I am certain that great things are in store for you. *You are going to reclaim your life!* This time, don't forget to take my phone number.' Vini chuckled as they got up to go.

'Thanks, Vini.' Jay felt much lighter as he hugged Vini.

Thanks for bringing me back to life . . .

Vini said, 'Call me tomorrow morning at 7 a.m.'
     Jay turned to go. Vini watched Jay as he walked
away. He remembered Ajaat's final words to him,

> *'Ja. Andheron mein thokar khaye huon ka*
> *chirag ban.'*

> 'Go. Be a lamp unto ones
> who are stumbling in the dark.'

16

The Balm of Forgiveness

Jay walked out of the mall slowly. He had decided to take the empty styrofoam coffee cup back with him. It was a grim reminder of his darkest moment, just an hour ago.

It was drizzling, and he turned his face upwards, feeling the water flow over his face and down his throat in rivulets. The water felt warm after the cold, air-conditioned mall. He sensed that all his unhappiness was being washed away. He felt like singing.

He saw the silvery edges of clouds as sunrays peeked through. There was a beautiful rainbow in the sky. 'Sun and rain together. Jackals are getting married,' his dad would have told him.

Jay laughed for the first time in months.

He slept well that night and woke up very early. Not due to any discomfort, but out of anticipation. His chance encounter with Vini was running through his mind when he awoke. He couldn't believe that he had been contemplating ending his life just moments before he heard Vini singing.

Day was breaking, and he could hear birds chirping. The violet hue to the east was telling him that the rain clouds were gone and that the day would dawn bright and sunny.

Happy birthday, Jayshankar Prasad.
Today is the first day of your second life.

Jay tried to make himself look presentable after months of apathy. He was going to meet the one man who could help him reclaim his life. He called Vini at 7 a.m., as directed. Vini told him to reach the mall entrance in ten minutes. Jay now realized that Vini also lived close by. Vini was going for his morning walk, and Jay was to join him.

'It took three months for me to run into you, Vini, although we've been living so close to each other,' Jay said.

'Everything comes about at the right time, Jay.' He sang,

'Miti dhund jag chaanan hoyaa,
Jio kar suraj nikaliyaa,
taare chhape andher paloaa'

'The fog has cleared and the world shines bright,
With the sun's appearance,
stars disappeared and darkness is driven away.'

'There's an ancient zen saying, "When the student is ready, the teacher appears." We both are ready to learn from each other now, I guess,' Vini said softly. Jay nodded in silence.

As they started walking, Vini asked, 'Did you have a good sleep?'

'Yes. But I woke up very soon.'

'That's okay. It's not only how long you sleep but how deep, without waking up time and again. Did you feel refreshed when you got up?'

'Absolutely,' Jay said.

Vini nodded. 'When we eat the right food and sleep well, we are energized. Our body and mind need to be taken care of properly, for us to remain healthy and happy. The body needs proper nourishment, as does the mind, Jay. But there are two other aspects that keep us energized. Exercise and meditation. Proper exercise is essential to keep the body healthy. Meditating regularly purges the mind of toxic thoughts and emotions, and keeps us happy. A calm and peaceful mind is the most important of all.'

Jay was deep in thought. 'Food, sleep, exercise and meditation. I haven't taken care of any of these, Vini.'

'Yes Jay, and this has led to your present state of misery. In your unaware and chaotic state of mind, you have nearly destroyed everything that you cherished, Jay. Health, family, friends, work and even your dreams.'

'So what do I need to do now, Vini? Everything is gone.'

'Not completely, Jay. There's still hope.' Vini smiled. 'But that's provided you want it back.'

'Of course I do, Vini! Please help me find the way,' Jay pleaded.

Vini nodded. He was silent as they trudged along. He remembered what Ajaat had mentioned in passing to him, on different occasions. *To learn anything worthwhile, a student must pass through four important filters.*

An ideal student must have an intense desire to learn, the capability to go through the rigours of transformation, sincere humility to seek guidance from an able teacher and perseverance to sustain till the goal is attained.

Jay was eager to heal, he had the physical and mental capacity, and he had made the request to Vini. Would he be able to persevere? There was no way to know until Jay tried. Vini had to take that call.

Ajaat had taken the same call with him . . .

The sun was coming up and it was getting warm. Jay noticed the rain-washed world around him for the first time. Sunlight filtered through the leaves of the trees, there was grass growing through cracks in the tiles on which they were walking. Flowers were blooming, and birds were singing.

Vini finally spoke, 'Jay, the first thing you will need to do is to heal the damage that's already done. When a house is on fire, we need to douse the flames immediately. Everything else can be done later.'

Jay was listening intently now. Vini continued, 'There's a beautiful annual tradition in the Jain community where one asks every person whom they might have offended for *michhami dukkadam* or forgiveness. It is very powerful. Old quarrels are forgotten and friendships are renewed through this act. This is the first thing you have to do, Jay, to personally go and ask for forgiveness from all the people that you have hurt.'

Jay stopped mid-stride. His heart was thumping hard, and his stomach lurched. 'Vini, I . . . I can't.' He felt panic at the very thought of facing his parents, Raghav and others. A frisson ran up his spine. How could he even face them? They didn't want to have anything to do with him at all.

Vini stopped walking. He turned and looked long and hard at Jay. 'I know you can, Jay. You would have died yesterday. *In a way, you did.* Think of that Jay as gone forever. He doesn't exist any more. So, who is this man who can't say sorry?' Vini didn't wait for Jay's reply and began walking again.

So he knew that I was going to end everything yesterday. Jay took deep breaths, and his panic began to subside. He was in a brown study. He began walking quickly and caught up with Vini.

Vini spoke firmly now. 'Secondly, you will need to ask them to tell you what they really think of you. Ask for both your positive and negative points. Finally, you need to ask for their advice on how you should improve. You will need to listen to them with deference, without reacting or trying to explain yourself,' Vini said, turning to look at Jay once more. 'Jay, if you want to reclaim your life, you will have to begin with this. And, rest assured that it is going to be tough.'

* * *

Jay reached Raghav's home and rang the bell. It was early evening, and he knew Raghav would be home. The door was opened by Raghav's seven-year-old daughter, Arushi. 'Jay Uncle!' She shouted happily, and they hugged, but Jay didn't step inside. Raghav came out, saw Jay and frowned. He told his daughter to go inside and, without a word, shut the door on Jay's face.

Jay knew Raghav was listening from behind the closed door and said, 'Rags, I know I don't deserve your friendship after all that I said. I have come to ask for your forgiveness. You are the only guy I can talk to, Rags. You were absolutely right about Ritika. She was a real gold-digger. She's out of my life. Can you ever forgive me? Please, Rags. I am really and truly sorry.' Tears rolled down Jay's cheeks, and he sniffled as he spoke. 'You are the only one who understands me. You are my yaar! I have really been a stupid fool, Rags, but really, I love you.'

The door opened, and Raghav rushed out and hugged Jay. He too had tears in his eyes. 'You have been a real bastard, Jay, but I have really missed you too!' Raghav said. 'Come in, and let's have hot chai and pakoras.'

They spoke for hours. Jay told Raghav about his depression and his suicidal thoughts. Raghav wept and hugged him again. Jay then told him about his fortuitous meeting with Vini and what he'd told him to do. Raghav realized that Jay was really sincere about making amends. 'Let me do something, Jay. I will try and organize another meeting of our group without mentioning you.'

Two days later, on Raghav's insistence, nearly all their friends came to the same club without knowing that Jay would be there too. Jay sat in an adjacent room, awaiting Raghav's signal. When he went inside, everyone was surprised and angry. Some even got up to leave. Raghav requested them to give Jay just ten minutes, as he had something important to share with them. The guys agreed and sat down.

Jay spoke haltingly. 'Guys, I am really sorry for that evening. I have been a real jerk. Today, I need your help. I know I don't deserve it. I'm sure you all know by now that I have lost everything. Money, family, your friendship, my health. Everything. But I haven't come to ask for financial help. I want you to tell me my flaws. I want your advice as to how I can become a better person.' The classmates looked surprised. A few looked pretty annoyed.

'Jay, please stop this drama. You always have some hidden motive behind your sweet talk. I can't trust you for even a single moment,' one guy spat out.

'Guys, I can vouch for Jay's sincerity,' Raghav intervened.

'Raghav, why are you taking the side of this piece of shit? I thought that you, of all people, would stay away from this snake in the grass!'

Raghav told them about Jay coming to meet him and his determination to turn his life around. He told them about Jay wanting to take his life. That calmed the friends a bit.

Soon, the classmates began sharing angry admonitions and made bitter accusations. They were talking over each other. This was followed by a lot of sensible advice and counsel from everyone, which Jay humbly accepted without reacting, as Vini had instructed.

Strangely, the tone changed as the evening progressed, and the classmates started doing the same exercise among themselves too. They opened up to each other and said things they wouldn't have under normal circumstances. Many of them became nostalgic and teased Jay, and each other, as they remembered their school days. Raghav joked about Jay falling for every pretty girl he saw. In the end, everyone was laughing, and a couple of them started singing the songs that they sang together in their school days. Everyone felt lighter, and they all told Jay that it had been one of the best evenings they'd had in a long time and that they must continue having such frank conversations. Most of the guys came and hugged Jay, who felt a million tonnes lighter.

Raghav concluded, 'Loyal, frank, sincere and dependable. That's who a real friend is. And, Jay, today you've proved that you are a true friend to me.'

* * *

Jay knew that his father went to the bank every Wednesday, as the crowd was thin in the middle of the week. He decided to wait for him outside the bank. Once Satish had completed his work at the bank, he walked out slowly. His shoulders were slumped, and he looked like he had aged ten years since Jay had gone away.

Jay followed him as he walked to his car. He called out to his father from behind. 'Dad!'

His father paused mid-stride and, without looking back, began walking again. Jay called out once again, but Satish didn't stop till he reached his car.

'Dad, please listen to me for just one minute. I have not come to cause trouble. Please, Dad. Just one minute.'

Jay's father stopped fiddling with the car keys and turned to face Jay. 'Jay, I don't really . . . Wha- . . . What happened to you? Are you okay?' Satish saw that his son looked sick and skeletal. Jay had lost so much weight that his clothes hung over his body.

'I am as okay as can be, Dad. How have you been? How is Ma?'

'We both are fine, Jay. Shubhra is worried sick for you. I . . . I am too, béta. Haven't you been eating? Where have you been staying?' Satish's words tumbled out. His concern had made him forget all his rancour.

Jay stood quietly. He felt like the eight-year-old who had sidled up to his dad to tell him that he had broken a neighbour's windowpane while playing cricket. His voice was choked with emotions and came out as a croak. 'I am really sorry, Dad. I have been a stupid idiot. I should have listened to you, and I would never have got into this mess.'

Jay's father walked to him and embraced his frail frame tightly. His eyes glistened with tears. 'What have you done to yourself, Jay? Why didn't you come back home?'

'I thought you were angry with me, Dad!' Jay sniffled. He, too, couldn't hold back his tears.

'You are my son, dammit! Everything I own is yours, béta! I am sorry that I was so harsh with you. Come home with me! Shubhra will be so happy to see you!'

'Only if you let me drive you home, Papa.' Jay hadn't called Satish 'Papa' since he had left for college.

Jay drove the car, and Satish sat next to him, wiping away his tears constantly. His prodigal son was coming back home. When they reached their house, Satish kept a finger on his lips, indicating to Jay that he wanted to surprise Shubhra. He went into the house quietly, telling Jay to wait outside, and called out, 'Shubhi! Can you please come outside? I need help in getting this inside. Hurry, please!'

Shubhra had just had a bath and had a white towel wrapped around her head. She came out in a hurry, looking slightly irritated. 'What is it? I was having a bath!' Suddenly, she saw Jay standing outside, grinning, and she broke into sobs. Satish had a look of delight on his face. All three hugged each other and went in. They talked throughout the day over gobhi parathas, mango pickle and pudina raita.

Satish soon became sentimental. 'Jay, somehow I believe that I am entirely to blame for all the mess in your life.'

'No, Dad, I became greedy. I wanted to get rich quickly,' Jay said earnestly. 'You both kept trying to knock sense into my head, but it was all my arrogance and stupidity.'

'That's true, son. You were extremely ambitious, and it led to disaster. But I failed you. I couldn't give you the right values. I don't really know where I went wrong.' Satish sighed.

'No, Dad, please. I have always admired you. You are my hero. This mess I am in is due to my own short-sightedness. I wanted to impress you both and to show off in front of everyone. I wanted to give you both things that I believed you should have. I wanted you to be one up on your own friends. I realized very late that you both are happy with whatever you have. Ma and you have always taught me that things don't make people happy, but I thought I was smarter than you both. I really have been so stupid,' Jay said quietly.

Shubhra said, 'Béta, it really doesn't matter. I am so grateful to god that he brought you back home safe and sound. Come back home, Jay. Stay with us.' Her eyes welled up once again. 'We really miss you, béta.'

'Ma, I think it would be better for me to stay on my own for now. It will be more convenient that way, I guess. I am sure I will set up a new business very soon. But I promise, I will come more often, now that I am back to being single!'

'Thank god that girl is out of your life, Jay. Truth be told, she was the worst of all your girlfriends,' Satish said.

'You never told me that!' Jay chuckled. 'And yes, I am a terrible judge of women, that I admit!'

'You would jump at my throat as soon as I mentioned her! We have spent three of the worst years of our lives because of that gold-digger! And you! Running around her like a puppy dog, all the time!' Jay's dad chuckled.

'Okay! Now, you both need to stop fighting. Thank goodness that she has gone. Good riddance!' Shubhra snorted. All three began laughing.

Jay's journey to reclaim his life had begun.

17

Clearing the Field

Jay decided to stay back at his parents' home for the night. Satish and Shubhra wouldn't let him out of their sight. After dinner, Shubhra followed Jay to his room and stood at the door, chattering nineteen to a dozen. He listened to her nodding occasionally as she filled him up on a lifetime of inane stories that he had never paid attention to. Tonight, he wasn't going to snap at her. He just wanted to hear his ma's happy voice. The words didn't matter at all.

Jay hadn't realized that Satish too had come up and was standing behind Shubhra, shielded by the wall along the door, until he interrupted her and told her that it was getting late and that they should let Jay sleep. Jay told them that it wasn't a problem at all. He asked them to sit on his bed with him, for the first time in more than fifteen years. Soon, Satish too was sharing stories, until he noticed that Jay's eyes were drooping. He got up immediately and told Jay to lie down. 'Béta, you must sleep now. It has been a very long day.'

Before they left, Shubhra stroked his forehead and kissed his hand lovingly. Satish, who wasn't very expressive, awkwardly tousled Jay's hair, something he'd not done since Jay was a little boy. 'Good night, Jay béta. May god bless you.'

Jay smiled to himself. He hadn"t felt this good about himself in many, many years. Somehow, it felt very different sleeping in his own bed. It was the bed he'd had since he was a teenager, but tonight it felt . . . more welcoming. The house, too, seemed alive. It felt warm and loving as he closed his eyes. He drifted into deep, dreamless sleep.

The next morning, rain clouds had parted, letting the sunlight through. Jay saw this as a sign that better days were in store for him. He decided to leave for Vini's home immediately after breakfast. Satish and Shubhra walked with him to the gate, and Jay smiled at its squeak. It sounded alive and happy as well.

* * *

Jay reached Vini's place within an hour. A set of narrow steps led up to Vini's first-floor tenement. Jay ran up nimbly and reached a wooden door with greenish paint chipping off it. He heard soft strains of the strumming of the ektara and Vini's sonorous voice seeping through the door.

'Milon hobey koto diney
aamaar mon-er maanush-er shoney.'

There was a blackened iron chain hanging over the door from a thick old nail, hammered into the warped and cracked wooden door frame. Jay couldn't see any bell.

'*Chaatoko praay ohornishi*
cheyey aachi kaalo shoshi.
Hobo boley chorono daashi
o to hoy naa kopaal guney.'

He saw a marked depression in the door shutter near the last link of the chain and guessed that the chain itself was used to knock on the door.

'*Megh-er bidyut meghey jemon*
lukaale naa paai anweshon.
Kaalaare haaraaye temon
o rup heri-e dorponey.'

Jay raised his hand to grip the chain and knock, but he stopped himself midway. He wanted to immerse himself in the soulful song and decided to sit on the steps.

'*Jokhon oi roop shorono hoy*
thakena loko lojjar-o bhoy.
Lalon fakir bhebe boley sodai
oi prem je kore se jaaney.'

The song was over, and the silence felt deep, velvety and comfortable. Jay sat quietly for a few minutes before he got up again, knocked softly and waited.

Vini opened the door moments later. He was delighted to see that Jay was back. 'Aah! There you are, Jay! Come in, sit down.'

Vini sat on a chataai spread on the ground. His ektara lay next to him. Jay, too, sat on the chataai after removing his shoes.

The room was frugally furnished. There was a wooden bed on one side. Next to it was an empty table and a single chair. The floor was rough-hewn stone that had smoothened with age. On the other side, there was an open window with green wooden shutters through which sunlight filtered into the room. There was a small kitchen with stainless steel utensils next to the window and a small gallery, which possibly led to a toilet at the back. Everything looked spotlessly clean.

'That was such a soulful song you were singing just now,' Jay said, looking thoughtful. 'But the words were in some unknown language.'

Vini smiled and nodded. 'That was a Baul song in the Bengali language. It is written by Lalon Shah, who was called the king of Bauls, who were the wandering fakirs of Bengal. In this song, he seeks union with his *Mon-er Manush*, the one who lives in his heart. Lalon sings here as Radha, who is pining for her Krishna. But, at a deeper level, Lalon is singing of the yearning of a seeker to attain the self.'

'When will I be united,
With the One who lives in my heart!

Day and night, like a Chaataka bird,
I thirst for the Dark Moon,

Yearning to serve at His feet
But that isn't my destiny.

Just as the flash of lightning, hiding in a cloud,
Which I cannot find, despite searching intently.
Thus, the Dark One has become obscured,
It is His visage I behold, looking in the mirror.

The instant I remember His form,
I am no more afraid of worldly shame.
Lalon the minstrel contemplates always,
That the one who loves thus, knows.'

Vini became quiet. He had his eyes closed. A soft smile
played upon his lips. He felt the words that he sang
deeply. Jay found the meaning of the song exquisite.
He waited until Vini opened his eyes.

'How do I thank you, Vini? So much has changed
in these last few days!' Jay said gratefully.

'I am so glad to hear that, Jay. I see that you are
looking better.' Vini smiled.

'I do feel energized. I have found love and
acceptance from my parents and friends once again.
It's all because of you.' Jay's voice was emotional.

'If you want to thank me, Jay, then follow what I
ask of you without fail. I promise you that it's going to
change your life.'

'Vini, you are my teacher, my guru. I owe you my
life. I trust you completely. I want to reclaim my life. I'll
follow all your instructions,' Jay said in a serious tone.

Vini's voice became grave. 'Jay, the road ahead will
be tough. At times, you'll want to quit. At times you'll

believe you have learnt everything you need to and you're done. But, you will be done only when I say so, Jay, not when you decide. If you are ready, then you need to give me your unconditional word.'

'I assure you that I will not quit.' Jay spoke sincerely. Vini nodded. He hoped so too. But only time would tell.

Jay looked as if he wanted to ask something. Vini encouraged him with a smile. 'Vini, can I ask you something? How long have you lived here?'

'Almost eight years.'

'You have travelled all around the world, I guess.'

'Yes, Jay. Possibly. I really don't keep track.'

'I don't see anything from your travels around the world, Vini. Where's your stuff? Your clothes, books, your luggage . . .'

'Where's yours, Jay?'

'Mine? But I don't live here!' Jay exclaimed.

Vini smiled compassionately. 'Neither do I, Jay . . .' he whispered. 'I am just travelling through.'

'Ye zameen musaafir khaanaa hai,
Hum do pal ke mehmaan hain . . .'

'This world is a traveller's lodge,
We are guests here for a couple of moments . . .'

Jay stared at Vini, nonplussed.

'Come, let's go. We have work to do.' Vini got up and began walking out the door. Jay followed him down the steps quickly.

Vini walked fast, and Jay was surprised at his energy. For nearly twenty minutes, they walked in silence on a dirt road through a village. They crossed a few fields before Vini stopped near a small piece of land filled with dry bushes, garbage and undergrowth. It appeared to have been neglected in contrast to the well-maintained fields all around. 'What do you see here, Jay?' Vini asked. His tone had become crisp, and he looked serious.

Jay was confused. 'I see a badly neglected plot of land. Maybe it doesn't belong to any of the farmers here. Could be disputed property.'

'This is you, Jay,' Vini said.

'I don't understand, Vini.'

'This little piece of land has not been cared for. It has the same potential as the land around it, but due to some legal issues it was left unattended for decades. The result is in front of us.'

'So how is this connected to me, Vini?' Jay pushed for an answer.

Vini didn't reply but continued talking about the land. 'One of my well-wishers requested me to meet the disputing parties to help them reach a compromise. To cut a long story short, they thought it best that I utilize the land as I saw fit.' Vini turned to Jay. 'And, I want you to make this field into a beautiful garden, Jay.'

Jay didn't know what to say. 'I . . . I will get it organized, Vini . . . I will call someone . . .'

'No, Jay. I want you to do everything yourself.'

Jay felt uncomfortable. 'I haven't ever done any farming, Vini. I really don't know . . .'

'You will, Jay. You will,' Vini said firmly. 'You need to start right away. If you want to leave, I won't stop you. But then, I will not be able to continue teaching you. We will meet at 1 p.m. for lunch, if you're still here. I will bring food for you.' Saying so, Vini turned to go.

'Vini, how do I do this? I don't have any tools!' Jay shouted to the rapidly disappearing Vini, who didn't turn around.

Jay stood feeling lost for a long time. The place was deserted. There was no one he could ask any help from. Slowly, he came to a decision and began picking up dried wood and stones, piling them on one end of the plot.

The land wasn't very large, possibly a hundred feet wide and double that in length, more triangular than rectangular, since it tapered towards the far end. Gradually, Jay began to organize the work in his mind and began cleaning systematically. He became so engrossed in his work that he didn't realize when Vini arrived.

Vini stood and watched Jay from afar quietly, until Jay spotted him. He didn't stop working, and Vini nodded in approval. 'You have done well, Jay. Come, wash your hands and let us eat.'

Jay's hands were scratched and bleeding. Vini tenderly cleaned the wounds. 'Do you know why we are doing this?'

Jay said, 'I guess it has to do with me, Vini.'

Vini said, 'We will talk after we eat.' He took out two small metal tins and gave one to Jay. Inside, there were 2 rotis, lightly cooked peas with potatoes and half an onion. Jay ate hungrily. It struck him that Vini must have cooked all this, and he felt grateful. The food tasted really good after his strenuous efforts in cleaning the field.

As Jay ate, he said, 'You had said that this land is like me. So, maybe I am doing this exercise to heal something within me.'

Vini nodded as they ate. He hardly ever talked while eating. After finishing the food, Vini took Jay's tin and kept it away with his own. 'This field represents the arena of our lives, Jay. Like it, you have neglected your own life for a long time. As you are cleaning this field, you have to clean your mind too.

'It takes a long time to make a field that yields a good crop. Before sowing the seeds, the farmer clears all the rocks, roots, garbage and dry wood from the land, just as you are doing right now. In the same way, your life field needs to be cleaned Jay.

'Over time, a lot of dirt and muck has accumulated in your life. You made a mess of things. Your relationships have mended a bit, but unless you work to keep them healthy, they may go downhill once more. We act without realizing that there are consequences for every action.'

'WYGIWYG,' Jay said. 'What you give is what you get.'

Vini laughed softly. 'You remember that one! Yes, that's exactly what has happened to you. You are now getting whatever you gave in the past.' Jay nodded.

'Good. Now you must get back to work. Clean this field as well as you can by evening. Then have a bath and come to meet me.' Vini got up to go.

Jay didn't call out as Vini left. He knew that he had to clear the field before dark.

Jay reached Vini's room a little after sunset. He felt exhausted but happy. His body ached, but some weight seemed to have lifted from his mind.

Vini gave him hot tea and began, 'Jay, cleaning must happen in different areas of your life simultaneously. Good health is *swasthya*, or being established in the self. Just cleaning the body and not taking care of one's mind is not sufficient. You need to take care of the place you spend most of your time in and what you imbibe. The environment needs to be conducive to the well-being of your mind and body.

'Remember, this body is the only place you'll live in all your life. You need to take care of it. Nourish the body with good food and keep it healthy through yoga and exercise. A healthy body houses a healthy mind.

'When your mind is healthy, you will feel good about yourself. You won't entertain negative thoughts. All your unhappiness will vanish. You will feel energetic and creative. You'll see opportunities instead of problems.

'When people are sad, they don't feel good about themselves. This leads to unhappy thoughts, which lead to lowered immunity and disease. Unhappy people usually have troubled relationships,' Vini concluded.

'I feel that when one is not at ease, one is not joyful,' Jay said.

'Absolutely. Disease is ill-health. An unhealthy person is called *a-swastha*, or one who isn't in touch with one's self. In other words, one isn't spiritual when one isn't healthy in all aspects,' Vini said.

It took Jay nearly two weeks to clear the field. It rained intermittently, and the ground was soft and easy to clear. With Vini's guidance, Jay soon began sorting out the mess his life was in. He cleaned out his room, started eating a healthy diet of fruits and vegetables, began to get his finances in order and started exercising every day.

Jay felt enthusiastic and proud of his achievement. 'Vini, I have cleared the field! I have cleaned up my life! Thank you so much. I feel really good!'

Vini watched his progress without judgement. He knew that tougher times were in store for Jay.

18

Patterns in the Mind

Over a month had gone by since Jay had cleaned the field, and the monsoon was in full swing. Vini insisted that Jay should keep cleaning the field and all other areas of his life repeatedly.

Soon, Jay began feeling frustrated, as he felt nothing much was happening. 'All Vini tells me is to keep cleaning. What more is left to clean? Haven't I cleaned everything? Vini doesn't even come to check on me. What's the point?'

Soon, this frustration began to show up as irritability, and some of his past anger began to reappear. One day, Vini came and inspected the field. He shook his head and told Jay to continue the task.

Jay frowned. 'I think that the field is perfectly clean and ready, Vini,' he declared. 'I guess you have saved some money through this exercise. I don't really have time to waste, you know. I am trying to set up a business, and this isn't helping at all. Anyway, all you do is sit in your room doing nothing, singing songs and playing the ektara. I really feel cheated, Vini. I had expected that you would guide me and help me rebuild my life. But, all you've done is to get me to personally clean your field repeatedly. I can get some farmer boy to do this for you. Do you think that I have no other work to do?'

Vini's face remained impassive. His eyes were filled with sadness as he noted that Jay's old patterns were back. He turned and left without saying a word.

Jay stood watching him go. He was scowling, and his breathing was jagged. He dug his nails into his palm and bit his lip till he could taste his own blood. His head was throbbing. He felt beads of sweat on his frowning forehead as he turned and began to walk quickly, wanting to put as much distance as he could between himself and the offensive man.

* * *

'Rags! Where are you? Can we meet?'

Raghav recognized the tension in Jay's voice immediately. It was tremulous and high-pitched.

'Jay, are you okay? Where have you been? It's been over a month.'

Jay didn't want to speak on the phone. He wanted to sit and talk with his friend. Raghav was at work, but he could sense that Jay really needed him. He decided to take a half-day to meet his friend.

'Jay, let's meet at the ashram at 1.30 p.m. I have some work there.' The ashram was a small hospice and gaushala, where destitutes and old cows were tended to by a small group of followers. The place wasn't very far from where Jay lived. Raghav's guru wasn't alive, but he used to go to the ashram regularly.

They met for a modest lunch at the ashram. Jay told Raghav all that had happened, agitatedly. 'Rags, things are really messed up, yaar. This new business venture hasn't worked out as I expected. Every investor wants quick returns, which means using unfair means. I've promised myself, Rags. I just cannot go that route again.' Jay stopped.

Raghav was a good listener and didn't interrupt. He knew this wasn't the real issue. Jay would come out with what was really bothering him soon enough. He simply nodded slowly.

Jay's voice had dropped an octave as he continued, 'On top of all this, Rags, Vini is being completely unreasonable. I can achieve so much more, if he stops wasting my time!'

Raghav caught Jay's changed tone as he spoke of Vini. Jay sounded hurt and betrayed. 'I think the issue here is Vini, Jay, not your new business. Isn't it?'

Jay's words came in a torrent. 'That man is so stuck up, Rags! We have been wasting so much time doing nothing at all. He's made me dig a bloody field up a hundred times, and he's still not satisfied! What does he want from me? Look at my hands, Rags, they have blisters. I am slogging my ass off trying to get a business going, and all I want from him is a little sympathy and understanding . . .'

'You've had a fight, haven't you?' Raghav cut him off uncharacteristically.

Jay pursed his lips. He was frowning as he nodded without making eye contact with his friend. 'I am not going back there, Rags. Enough is enough.'

Raghav had a faraway look on his face. He didn't speak for a long time. Jay fiddled with his food without eating it and finally pushed his plate away. 'Come on, Rags, say something. And don't tell me to go back to Vini, please.'

Raghav spoke almost in a whisper, 'You remember when we first met at school, Jay? We were ten years old. I had come to live with Mamaji, my mother's younger brother. My father had died a few months before that. Maai used to get epileptic fits and needed a lot of care. My younger sister Nandita and I were too small. Our uncle had generously taken us all in, and your parents made me feel part of a happy family.' Raghav took a deep breath and asked, 'Do you know what *anaath* means, Jay?'

Jay had calmed down listening to Raghav. He wasn't ready for the question. 'Wha- . . . anaath? It means an orphan, Rags.'

Raghav nodded. 'By the time I turned twelve, Maai had also passed on, as you know, and I was anaath, Jay. But, my uncle was a good man. He never made us feel anaath in any way.'

Raghav stood suddenly, picking up the plate of uneaten food. 'Come with me.'

Jay followed him meekly, carrying his own plate. Wordlessly, Raghav put the food in a refuse bin, and Jay followed suit. They washed their utensils, and Raghav silently led the way into the sanctum sanctorum of the ashram. This semi-dark room was where his guruji had lived over a hundred years ago. A faded black-and-white photograph of the master was kept on a wooden cot, and a small diya was kept burning there. Raghav bent down and respectfully paid his respects by touching his forehead to the ground in a *pranaam*. Jay followed. He had come to the ashram with his friend hundreds of times ever since they had been young boys. But, today, he saw a very different Raghav, who appeared pensive and sombre.

'Jay, I am both fortunate and unfortunate. Fortune favoured me when my uncle brought me to Guruji. I have only known him through this picture and this ashram. He left no teachings, but his loving grace has always provided all the strength I have needed to go through life. And yet, I feel extremely unfortunate because I never got to meet my spiritual master in flesh and blood. But Jay, once I came to my guru, I knew that I wasn't anaath anymore. My guru became my father, mother, friend and protector. I *knew* that I was never going to be alone, ever again . . . How strange it is, Jay, that you have chosen to make yourself spiritually bereft—an anaath. You have a living guru, and yet, you have walked out on him, choosing to insult and ridicule his ways of teaching you.'

Jay was aghast. Raghav continued, 'Jay, the guru's methods are unfathomable. He won't provide you the sympathy you crave. A guru isn't here to give us what we want. Often, what we want isn't good for us. We are ordinary mortals, who don't have any idea of what we really need for our good. The guru knows what you need, Jay, and he ensures that is what you gain by remaining in his grace.'

Raghav sighed. 'I pity you, Jay. You have let your pride and ego win. If you had even the slightest understanding of the immense sacrifice your guru has made for your welfare, you will not be able to live with yourself for a single moment.'

> '*Ye tan vish kee belaree, guru amrit kee khaan.*
> *Sheesh diyo jo guru mile, to bhee sasta jaan.*'

> 'This body is a vine,
> replete with many worldly poisons,
> Guru is the fount of the nectar of immortality.
> Giving up the pride-filled head,
> if one attains one's guru,
> Know it to be a truly cheap bargain!'

Saying this, Raghav turned and walked out of the ashram without looking back. Jay stood tongue-tied, staring at his friend's rapidly receding figure.

* * *

Jay got back to his room and sat down. He was feeling thoroughly confused. Raghav seemed to know Vini better than him. The guru's ways are truly inscrutable.

What had Vini done to him!

He looked into the old mirror hanging in his room. He had cleaned the plastic frame thoroughly, just days ago. The man who looked back at him appeared physically healthy, but extremely unhappy. The face was in a snarl.

He stared into his reflection's eyes. He could sense loathing. He wanted to look away, but something kept his gaze locked into those eyes, filled with disgust.

Nothing can save you, Jay . . . You are pathetic.

The man in the mirror quickly began to blur and dissolve. And, in his place Jay saw Vini's saddened eyes looking at him.

Jay realized that he was crying. He felt terrible about his uncontrolled outburst. Hot tears began rolling down his cheeks. They felt like molten lava, burning deep into his soul. He covered his face in his palms, and soon, he was shaking with painful, racking sobs.

The entire sequence of his meeting Vini at the Mall, on the fateful day when he was ready to end his life, flashed before his eyes. He felt nauseous and began to retch. He vomited acid, as he realized the enormity of what he had done. He looked up, into the mirror, once again. His image was looking back at him with compassion.

Softly, Jay and his image began to chant a couplet by Kabir that he had learnt at school.

'Guru govind do-u khade, kaake lagun paaye?
Balihari guru aapane govind diyo bataaye!'

'Who must I bow down to first,
when my guru and God stand before me?
Glories to you, my master,
for you have shown me God!'

Jay wiped away his tears with the back of his hand. *Oh Jay*, he heard Vini whispering to him at the mall. *Why have you done this to yourself?* He remembered Vini's hand on his head, tousling his hair. He looked up slowly. His world was a blur once more. But these tears were different. They were cleansing him.

Jay got up and rushed out of his room. It was drizzling. He ran all the way to Vini's home through the rain. He pleaded to be let inside, but Vini didn't open the door. 'I am really sorry, Vini,' Jay mumbled, his face pressed against the wooden door. 'God only knows what keeps coming over me. I cannot seem to help it. I choose the wrong company, and I keep losing my temper. I really don't know what to do, Vini.' Jay wept, but Vini remained firm.

'I won't leave until you forgive me, Vini. I will sit here all day and night,' Jay said as he sat down on the steps outside Vini's door.

Vini didn't respond. He had expected Jay to go through this difficult phase. Jay's sincerity and perseverance were being tested. If he came through, then Vini would be able to actually mould Jay into something beautiful. If Jay failed, then Vini wouldn't be able to teach him any further. This was the time Vini couldn't afford to ease up at all.

Jay sat on the steps all evening as rain dripped from the roof on to the steps and the landing. He wasn't going to move, he had decided. Whenever Vini came out, he wanted to seek his forgiveness. Vini had given him his life back. He had every right to make Jay do what he believed was necessary for Jay's well-being.

'Would you like a paratha, Jay béta?' Shubhra's gentle voice wafts up to him.

Jay is seated on a rocky outcrop, and far below him is the choppy sea. In front of him, the sun is about to set, and the sky is golden, orange and crimson. There are noisy seagulls flying around.

Shubhra is sitting next to him, and she has a gobhi paratha in her outstretched hand. Her face is unclear. But he knows it is her. Jay reaches out for the paratha. Suddenly, a squawking seagull swoops down and snatches it out of his hand. The head of the seagull morphs into the face of Shyam, cackling away loudly.

Shubhra, who has also transformed into a seagull momentarily, cries out in shock as her wings do not unfold and flap, hard as she tries. She looks terrified and screams as she falls off the cliff.

Seagull Satish appears out of nowhere and stretches out his wings. He catches Shubhra, who holds his wing by her claws. Then, Satish too leaps off the outcrop. Shubhra laughs as her wings open up. They both begin to fly in the sky, circling around Jay, laughing and beckoning to him. 'Come on, Jay, don't be afraid!' Satish calls out.

Jay reaches out to them when suddenly, seagull Ritika pushes him off the cliff, laughing sinisterly. Seagull Raghav swoops in and attacks Ritika fiercely as Jay loses his balance and slips off the outcrop. Shubhra, Satish and Raghav dive down and try to prevent his fall, while Shyam and Ritika swoop in and keep pecking at him. Jay cannot flap his wings, hard *as he tries. They are stuck to his sides. He starts falling very fast and rapidly leaves all of them behind.*

Jay screams out in fear as he falls faster and faster to certain death on the sharp rocks below. He sees that all the seagulls are now far away, high up, and he is plummeting all alone. He is going to hit the ground any moment. The world is a blur . . .

Suddenly, he feels a huge talon dig deep into his back, drawing blood as it grabs him. With a jerk that tears skin off his back, he stops falling. Jay finds himself suspended, inches above the craggy ground.

He looks up. Against the bright sun and clear blue sky, Jay sees that he is in the grip of a massive eagle, with magnificent outstretched wings, hovering over him. Its head gradually begins to morph into Vini's visage, and it speaks in a thunderous yet loving voice. 'Do not worry, Jay. I am here . . .'

But Jay has already begun slipping out of Vini's safe talons.

Time is running out . . .

Jay realized that he was tumbling down the steps as he awoke with a start. He hit his forehead on the wall and cried out in pain.

Vini heard the thudding sound and Jay's cry, and leaped up. It was 3.15 a.m. He opened the door and saw Jay lying at the bottom of the steps, groaning. It was a funny sight, and Vini laughed as he came down to help Jay get on his feet. Jay, too, saw the funny side of his predicament and chuckled as he winced due to the rapidly growing bump on his forehead.

'You are wet. Come and dry yourself,' Vini said quietly. He supported Jay as they walked up the wet steps. Jay didn't speak. The dream was still running through his head. Vini stopped and caught his breath at the landing. Rainwater was seeping through the walls at a few places. At one spot, the roof was leaking. 'Do you see that, Jay?'

'What, Vini?' Jay looked where Vini was pointing at the roof. 'I don't see anything.'

'Do you see that the roof is leaking, Jay?' Vini asked softly. Jay nodded. 'You have to stop the leak. Can you do it right now?' Vini asked.

'I can try, but I think it would be difficult as the walls are wet. We could put a bucket . . .'

'*You cannot repair a leaking roof when it is raining, Jay,*' Vini cut him off. 'You have to wait for the rain to stop.'

Jay didn't reply.

'You are in the same situation, Jay,' Vini said gravely. 'And if you don't get out of the rain of your present predicaments, you will be in very deep trouble.'

Jay stared at the leaking roof and tried to correlate what Vini was saying with his life. Vini was absolutely right. He was unable to manage himself. His life was careening out of control once more.

Vini asked him, 'Jay, have you ever thought about why you keep slipping back? You seem to like being in a situation where you don't have to take any responsibility for your well-being. Do you really want to get better at all?'

Jay could not answer. He felt frustrated with himself. He realized that he liked being an object of people's sympathy. He wanted them to ask him about his well-being again and again. It gave him a sense of self-worth and of being wanted. He knew that it stemmed from his need for his dad's love and admiration.

'I do, Vini,' he said in a small voice. 'Please help me. I don't want to be this way. I am really sorry for having said those things to you.'

Vini shook his head. 'Often, we get upset at things we cannot understand.'

'Bazeecha-e-atfal hai duniya mere aage,
Hota hai shab-o-roz tamasha mere aage . . .
Hum-pesha-o-hum-mashrab-o-humraaz hai mera,
Ghalib ko bura kyun kaho achchha mere aage . . .'

'This world seems a playground for children
in front of me,
Night and day, this grand show plays out
before me . . .
We are peers, we drink together, he's my confidant,
Why talk ill of Ghalib?
Do say that he is a good man,
To my face, at least . . .'

Jay sat still, trying to understand the words.

'These songs and couplets talk about you and me, and all humanity, Jay. They are pregnant with eternal truths. You will understand when the time is right. Don't worry, I am not upset with you. Just a little disappointed. Maybe I pushed you too hard, too fast. Right now, go home and rest. We will meet at the field tomorrow afternoon, as soon as the rain stops,' Vini said as he stuck a Band-Aid over the bruise on Jay's forehead.

The rain didn't stop all of the next day, and they met at the field the morning after. It was looking clean, and Jay felt proud of his handiwork. Vini looked sombre as he sat on his haunches and inspected the ground. Small and tender shoots were coming up in the wet and fertile earth. He shook his head as he stood up.

'This field is like our mind, Jay. Do you see the tender green shoots sprouting out of the ground? These are weeds and unwanted grass. These are just like the deep-seated tendencies of anger, greed, jealousy, lust, attachment, etc., within us.

'You have cleared the field so many times Jay, but these stubborn weeds keep growing back as soon as they receive nourishment from rain and the sun. In the same way, our deep-rooted habits and tendencies lie hidden underneath a calm exterior. Given suitable nourishment, these appear unbidden, and cause havoc in our lives.

'A good farmer knows that if he plants seeds in a field where weeds are growing, then he cannot expect a good harvest. The weeds would overrun the field and draw out all the nourishment from the field. His desired crop will surely wither away and die. Thus, he must ensure that the land is free of all such undesirable growth before he sows his crop.

'You have to do a lot of work on the field of your mind Jay. All your impulses are nothing but weeds in your mind. You constantly need to prevent weeds and garbage from piling up in your mind's field.'

Jay was in deep thought. He hadn't expected that the field hid so much under the surface. His mind was worse than this field. The filth he carried in it had destroyed his entire life. 'Vini, how do I clean my mind of harmful tendencies?'

'You must clear the field of every last weed, Jay. Even a single one can infest the field once again. In the same way, even one unwelcome tendency in you will spread like an uncontrolled wildfire throughout your mind. Negative thoughts and feelings breed constantly when you feed even a single one of them. People find pleasure in hurting others, because they have been hurt, some time. It's said that "hurt people *hurt* people".'

'I have hurt a lot of people, Vini, but today I can see that the person I have really hurt the most, was myself,' Jay said quietly.

Vini nodded. 'Yes, Jay. It's said that holding on to anger is like grasping a hot coal with the intent of throwing it at someone else; you are the one who gets burnt. The journey to heal yourself is going to be long. You will have to persevere. You cannot leave it midway. You have to give me your word.'

'Yes, Vini, I give you my word,' Jay said solemnly.

This time he knew that he would not quit.

19

The Commune

Jay lay on the chataai in Vini's room and listened to the pitter-patter of the rain hitting the tin roofs of adjacent houses. Vini watched over him from his cot. He remembered his second night at Ajaat's hut and smiled to himself. Despite having guided dozens of people, Vini felt special affinity with the young man. He drifted off to sleep.

Ajaat and Ash are walking in the forest. Ajaat is smoking his beedi. He points to a tree and Ash looks at it. There are ripe mangoes hanging from it. But as Ash goes close he realizes that they are pods. In each of the pods, a human is asleep in a foetal position. A foetus stirs, and Ash reaches towards it. Ajaat catches his outstretched hand and stops him.

'We never do that, béta. It will ripen on its own.' He points to the earth below the tree.

Ash now realizes that many of the pods have fallen to the ground. Most of them are rotting, and a putrefying stench emanates from them. Worms have eaten through many of them. He sees a few decaying foetuses struggling to get out of their pods. As he peers, one of them reaches towards him, wailing. Its little hand is covered in slimy mucus.

Ash cringes and pulls back. The foetus wails pitifully. It begins to melt and change form.

'The fallen ones often burst open. Maybe then, you should reach out to the ones who need help . . .' he hears Ajaat say. 'And that slime is going to be a part of it. You cannot avoid it, son.'

Ash gingerly reaches out to the wailing, slippery foetus. Its small fingers grab at Ash's hand. Ash gently grasps the hand as the foetus finally morphs into a miniature version of Jay. The slime begins to cover Ash as he pulls Jay out of the pod. Stringy slime still keeps him stuck, and Ash gives a jerk to free him. Jay cries out in pain, calling him, 'Vini, Vini . . .'

'Vini, Vini!'

Vini jerked his eyes open. Jay was standing in front of him, holding a cup of steaming hot chai.

'I couldn't find the ginger.' Jay smiled. 'Don't worry. Everyone says that I make good tea.'

Vini sat up slowly, smiling. It had been a lifetime since someone had woken him up and served him tea. It was actually pretty late in the morning, almost 8 a.m. He had slept like a log. But he realized that Jay hadn't.

'Thank you, Jay.' He took a long sip. 'Aah! This is really nice.'

'The rain has stopped. Should I go and work on the field today?'

'No, Jay. Go back to your room and pack some clothes for a few days.'

'Are we going somewhere, Vini?'

'Yes. As soon as possible. You need to disengage from worldly activities if you want to manage your life, Jay. Right now, your condition is as if a torrential rain is falling on you right now. You need to get out of the rain. I think it would be best for you to retreat from all non-essential activities for a while. No phones or emails. We will go out of the city to a quiet place for a few days. We should leave early, tomorrow morning.'

Jay agreed immediately.

'I will book a car to take us,' Vini said.

'Can I do that, Vini? I love driving. And, it's been a while.'

'We are going to Dehradun, at the foothills of the mountains. It will be a long drive, Jay, and you haven't slept all night.'

'I'll sleep in the day, Vini. Please let me do this!' Jay sounded like an eager young boy. Vini nodded and agreed.

* * *

'When a car is moving too fast, would you accelerate further to bring it under control?' Vini questioned Jay.

They had been on the road for almost an hour, having left before daybreak to beat the rush of city traffic. Jay was refreshed, and Vini remained quiet to let him concentrate on the driving. He watched the streetlights go off just before they turned on to the highway. The crimson sky looked beautiful, auguring a happy and fruitful journey. Jay had broken through a major barrier by taking this trip. Most people don't have the resolve to make a clean break from the world that they are entangled with. This was a good sign.

'That would be crazy, Vini. We must brake and slow down, otherwise we will crash,' Jay replied.

Vini nodded. 'The ancients likened our body with a *rath*, a chariot. The mind as the horses pulling it, and the soul as the charioteer. You are the driver of your life's rath, Jay. Right now it's moving helter-skelter and needs to be brought under your control.'

'My car seems to have a couple of punctures as well!' Jay laughed sheepishly as he drove on.

Vini smiled and added, 'A and B. Accelerator and Brake. Both are important to drive well, isn't it? Unlike a car, we can accelerate out of control in a number of ways. Each of these requires a different kind of braking. And, we must know when to accelerate, and when to apply brakes.'

'Wow. That is so apt. I have been racing along like a headless chicken, Vini. I really need to slow down.'

Vini agreed,

'*Dheere dheere re mana, dheere sab kucch hoye,*
Maali seenche sau ghara, ritu aaye phal hoye . . .'

'Slow down, slow down, dear mind,
everything occurs slowly,
A gardener may water the garden
with a hundred pots,
but fruits arrive only in their season . . .'

'How do I do this, Vini? I feel my entire life is careening out of control. It feels as if this car called Jay is hurtling downhill, and the brakes have failed. I am surely going to crash.' Jay sounded worried.

'Yes, Jay. And you will get to learn the way to deal with this soon enough. This place we are going to, is especially useful for letting you slow down the pace of your life.'

The road was getting crowded, and Jay constantly needed to be on the lookout as they passed small townships. A stray dog, a couple of milk vans, a fruit seller, a flurry of scooters, an impatient young driver in an open jeep honking continuously till he could overtake, a slow truck in front that didn't give them way, numerous police checkposts, long lines at toll booths and a myriad of unfilled potholes, all frustrated Jay, who cursed occasionally. Vini noticed his agitation growing, and suggested a break for relieving themselves and a quick breakfast.

As they sat down at a roadside dhaba, Jay remained restless. The irritation and stress of the drive was still troubling him. Vini said, 'Our mind holds on to negative emotions, and they linger for a long time, and unless we learn to drop these, they begin to harm our body. Much of illness manifests within us because we cannot manage our mind, Jay.'

'So what do I do, Vini? These guys have no respect for us, who follow rules. They just decide to leap on to the road, unmindful of their own safety, and ours. Bloody idiots!' Jay cursed.

Vini remained unperturbed. 'As you know, our thoughts create our actions. A positive mind creates positive actions, whereas an unclean mind creates undesirable actions. Situations cause us to react or respond. To control the mind, we need to curb its undesirable impulses, by applying brakes on ourselves constantly.'

'How can I do this?' Jay asked eagerly.

'To do this, Jay, one needs to avoid violence in thought, word and action.'

'And, how do I do that?'

'You'll need to force yourself to stop the urge to react.'

'True. I cannot seem to control the torrent of words and actions, Vini.'

'You'll need to control the tongue, Jay. Keep a check on your tongue and you will find a lot of peace,' Vini added.

Jay was pensive. His troubles had often been caused because of his outbursts. As they got in the car, he resolved to keep quiet throughout the next phase of the journey.

Vini was happy to see Jay consciously restraining himself. This was a sign of his resolve. Vini, too, kept silent and meditated in the car, until Jay parked near a food court for lunch. They were nearly halfway through their journey.

Vini called for a light lunch for both of them. Jay noticed that the man at the pay counter had cheated Vini and misappropriated hundred rupees. He pointed it out, and the man quickly apologized. He sheepishly gave the money back. Jay wanted to complain to the management, but Vini led him back to their table.

'We cannot sort out the entire world, Jay. But we can manage ourselves. There's an ancient practice of non-stealing which is very important for our work ethic and takes us ahead on the path. This man stole hundred rupees and was called out by you. But I can tell you, when I was Ashwini, I stole so much more than just money.'

'I don't understand.'

'Jay, just not stealing money doesn't make us honest. When you take something that isn't yours to take, you are stealing. Misappropriating anything—lying and enjoying comforts unfairly, plagiarizing ideas, wasting people's time, using people emotionally—all this is stealing.'

Jay was deep in thought now. Through bribery, he had acquired a number of projects. But had he really given up misappropriating completely? He would need to introspect deeply on that.

Vini added, 'See, if you become a slave to pleasure, you will become obsessed by or addicted to things that excite the senses. And you will want stuff that you can easily do without. This will make you steal. When you can avoid possessiveness, you will stop stealing.'

Jay looked confused. Vini explained as they finished their lunch and walked towards the car.

'Have you noticed that when we find something appealing, we want to possess it? We want to own experiences. Often, people want to visit places just to mark them off a list. Some look at a beautiful painting and desire it. Lustful people with uncontrolled urges can commit terrible crimes of passion. Desire brings up possessiveness. Often, possessive people do not share what they own and have unhealthy relationships.'

Jay nodded in understanding. 'Our greed begins with possessiveness, I guess. We begin to accumulate more than we need, and we hurt so many people when we become possessive.'

'Very well said, Jay. These different brakes can help slow down the hurtling car of your life.'

Soon, the roads began to narrow. A gradual climb indicated that they were approaching the foothills. The air started getting cooler. Vini asked Jay to shut off the air-conditioning and open the windows. They breathed the crisp and clean air deeply, and felt refreshed.

Jay said, 'Such a difference in the quality of air in the mountains! The pollution in the cities destroys our health completely.'

Vini nodded. 'Yes. You know, Jay, our cities are essential for the nation's development, and yet they are full of pollutants. We can come to the mountains, but then, we cannot manage an urban lifestyle here. People who work in cities don't realize the damage being done to their minds and bodies. It's a good idea to go to an unpolluted place once a year to recharge ourselves. But, we need to create healthy practices while living in the city, too.'

'How do we do that, Vini?'

'Healthy lifestyle practices bring harmony. We need to embrace cleanliness as a habit. When our environment is clean, our mind is joyful. Wear clean clothes and sleep on a clean bed. Steer clear of people who complain and gossip. Their unclean thoughts harm a purified mind.'

'I don't much enjoy the company of people who talk ill of others nowadays,' Jay said.

'That's a good sign, indicating that your practices are working, Jay,' Vini acknowledged. 'Another thing that helps is the practice of minimalism. If something doesn't serve you, let it go. Do not hold on to things for sentimental reasons or because they have monetary value, although they are useless to you.'

'Yes. By observing how you live, I began discarding stuff long ago. Not much remains to be cleared now.' Jay smiled.

Vini continued, 'Many people declare that they don't have the time for meditation and exercise. A healthy lifestyle actually frees up your time. Ensure that you utilize this time in exercise and meditation. It'll help you purge unhealthy social habits like late-night partying and wasting time on social media.'

'Aasan maare kya bhaya, mari na man ki aas,
Jyon kolhu ke bail ko ghar hi kos pachaas.'

'What is gained by doing asanas
when desires of the mind haven't yet died out?
It's like a plodder ox that travels a hundred miles,
turning the crushing wheel
while remaining at home!'

As the sun was setting, Vini and Jay arrived at a beautiful cottage at the foothills of the Himalayas.

It stood on the slopes of a verdant river valley, near a village, not too far from the city of Dehradun. The cottage was owned by Vini's friend Chandan, who had been only too happy to offer it to him. It was a part of a community of like-minded people, who lived either at the commune, or came and went, like Chandan.

The cottage was on two levels, with a garden on the undulating ground. A couple of wrought-iron benches painted turquoise blue were placed there, facing the Doon valley. Lush green grass and cobbled pathways led downwards to a babbling brook that flowed into the river below. Daffodils and chrysanthemums were in bloom all along the pathways. Jay came to know that Chandan, who did not live there, had also been groomed by Vini some years ago and was happy to share his place whenever Vini required it for guiding someone, like Jay, to reclaim their life. It was only then that Jay realized that there were many others like him, whom Vini had groomed over the years. Jay was put up with a number of other members of the commune, in a dormitory, a little distance away from the cottage.

Once they were settled in, Vini and Jay met at dinner. Vini's tone was serious and firm now. 'Jay, the first thing we need to do is to make your body healthy once again. Alongside, the mind too requires healing. The commune follows a strict regimen. All these will help manage the mind and body. A team of volunteers will take you through the daily timetable.'

Starting the next morning, Jay began a rigorous routine of getting up before sunrise and doing physical workout, followed by yoga asanas, breathing exercises and meditation. He was put on a strict diet of fruits and vegetables, and lightly cooked food, low on spices and in a measured quantity, by the commune's doctor.

During the day, Jay helped at an orphanage and an old-age home located nearby. He was also assigned to the community kitchen and to till the fields where organic produce was grown. This produce sustained the commune and was sold in the city. The money generated was utilized in running various service projects.

Jay did yoga asanas, breathing exercises and meditation once again around sunset, and had dinner soon afterwards. After this, everyone sat together and talked about something insightful to contemplate upon. Vini called this satsang, or the association with the wise. This was followed by an eight-hour sleep so that one woke up rejuvenated for the next day. No one watched television or used phones. In case of an emergency, one communicated with their family through the administration. Vini rarely met Jay at the commune. He left after a couple of weeks, while Jay stayed on.

* * *

It took Jay a long time. He followed Vini's instructions sincerely. As time passed, his mind became purified, and his body became stronger. He became quieter and more at peace with himself.

Winter came and went. Jay didn't go back to the city.

Nearly one year passed this way. Vini went abroad for the Mystic Music Festival in San Francisco. Once he was back, he permitted Jay to visit his parents and Raghav for a day. They were astonished at his transformation. Jay's hair had grown long and fell over his shoulders. He appeared wiry and lean, but not skinny. His face glowed with peace. Raghav was overjoyed at seeing his dearest friend. Satish and Shubhra wanted him to stay for a few days, but Jay said he couldn't. There was a lot of work to be done, and he would come back once he was permitted to do so by Vini.

* * *

One day in early spring, Vini came to the commune and called for him. 'You have done well, Jay. Now, you must leave the commune and continue these practices at home.'

Jay asked, 'I will do as you say. But will I be able to, Vini?'

'Jay, none of these practices are useful unless you interact with the world. When you live and work in the city, you'll interact with people and encounter different situations. Your natural reactions would arise unbidden. It is only at such times that you will be able to work further on yourself. You cannot grow any more if you continue to stay locked in the commune.'

* * *

Jay left the commune after another month, having completed thirty months there. Once he returned, he began working on the field once again, weeding it. This time he found it much easier to clear it, and soon it was ready for planting seeds.

Vini told Jay, 'Just as baby saplings need protection from harsh climate, scavengers and pests, the seeds that you plant in your mind also need a lot of care and protection. These will slowly grow into strong trees, Jay. And then, no hail or storm would be able to harm you.'

Jay agreed humbly. He felt astounded when he tried to fathom the immense effort Vini had put in, to making him whole again.

Vini wanted the field to be made into a garden where people could meditate. 'A beautiful garden soothes the senses and creates an atmosphere for peaceful introspection,' he said.

Jay started working night and day on the garden. He forgot to eat and often lost track of time. His health suffered. Vini noticed his zeal and appreciated it. But he wasn't too happy.

'Jay, passion is good for things that serve others and bring joy to the world. But, not at the cost of your well-being. You need to have compassion for yourself. Do not become obsessed or too hard on yourself.'

'Vini, I don't want to fail you this time. I will never be able to forgive myself if I am unable to do this one task you have given me, to your complete satisfaction.'

'You will always falter, Jay. We all do. And it's okay to fail when we are giving our one hundred percent. We aren't machines. But, remember that you must remain diligent and honest with yourself.'

'Yes, Vini. I realize that I need to love myself unconditionally. You keep telling me that. I often become hard on myself. I get really frustrated, because I don't see myself growing in ways that I have seen others progressing at the commune,' Jay said.

'How can one apply yardsticks to progress on this path, Jay? Never compare yourself with another person on the spiritual path. It's not a competition. Each of us grows at a different pace, isn't it? A mango tree and a coconut tree planted on the same day will bear fruit at different times and in different seasons,' Vini asserted.

Jay nodded slowly. He knew this but found it tough to imbibe. He resolved to be gentler on himself.

'We all must realize that there's a power greater than us that has created everything. Even your failings. You must make it a constant practice to surrender to this higher power and accept that everything cannot be in your control,' Vini concluded.

Jay simply said, 'Thank you. I am really fortunate that I have lived up to your trust in me. For me, you are the highest, Vini. You are my teacher and guru. I surrender myself to you.'

'Chaap tilak sab chheeni re mose nainaa milaaike,
Baat adham keh deeni re mose naina milaaike.'

'You have wrested my form, identity, and all else by gazing into my eyes.

You have spoken the inexpressible,
with just a glance.'

Saying so, Jay bowed down to Vini, his friend,
philosopher and guide. He had tears of gratitude
flowing from his eyes.

Vini hugged him. 'Welcome home, my dearest Jay.'

20

Go Forth and Embrace the World

'*Aamaay bhaashaaili re, aamaay dubaaili re,*
Okuul doriaar boojhi kuul naai re.
Kuul naai kinaar naai, naai ko doriaar paare
Shaabdhaane chaalaaiyo maajhi
aamaar bhaanga tori re.
Okuul doriaar boojhi kuul naai re.'

'I have been set adrift by you,
I have been drowned by you.
The endless ocean doesn't seem to have a shore.
There's no bank, there's no shore,
the ocean doesn't have limits.
Be cautious as you steer, O boatman,
my boat is a broken one.
The endless ocean doesn't seem to have a shore.'

Jay was mesmerized. 'What does the song mean, Vini?'
'Life is likened to an ocean with high and low tides
by the Bhatiyali mystic boatmen of Bengal. We are all

like damaged boats floundering in turbulent seas, Jay, and this world is a vast ocean—shoreless, endless and fathomless. The boatman is the wise guide or higher power that takes one across this life.'

Jay became silent, contemplating his own life. One more year had passed, and Jay had become proficient in the methods taught to him by Vini. His life had been full of upheavals, and until he had met Vini, he too had been floundering in the fathomless ocean.

'How are you sleeping nowadays?' Vini asked, breaking Jay's reverie.

Jay hadn't given this a thought for a long time. 'Very well, Vini. In fact, I hardly dream any more. And I get up refreshed.'

Vini nodded. 'That's a sign of good health. Sleep energizes us. As do proper nourishment, yoga, physical exercise and a positive state of mind. Continue the practices you learnt here. Share this precious knowledge with people who need guidance and lead them on to the path of wisdom. This world needs more good and happy people, Jay.'

'Where am I going?' Jay asked, confused.

Vini didn't respond. He asked Jay another question instead. 'Do you know what it means to be successful, Jay?'

'I think real success is not in how much we have achieved, but how far we will go to help others,' Jay said.

Vini nodded. 'True success can be measured by the number of smiles you bring to people in distress and the tears you wipe from unhappy faces.'

'You have done that for me, Vini, and I am eternally grateful to you. I don't know if I can ever repay you for turning my life around.'

'You can, Jay. By transforming others. So many people need guidance. There is a lot of work to do. You are ready to go and rebuild your life now, Jay.'

'My life is here, with you, Vini,' Jay insisted.

'Not any more, Jay. Boats aren't built to stay on the shores. A teacher only succeeds when his students spread out in the world and become teachers in their own right. This is the guru *parampara*, or the sacred teaching tradition. You have learnt everything that you needed to, Jay.'

'Go forth and embrace the world.
With the wisdom that you have gained,
Make your life beautiful.
Attain real success and peace.
Bring joy and happiness wherever you go.
That's a blessing, as well as an order.'

Jay said, 'I knew this day would come, but I feel lost, Vini. The life I left behind seems like another lifetime. I'll feel like a fish out of water.'

'Yes, Jay. That's the great test. You have to get back to the world and lead a worldly life once again.'

'Traverse the world like a dewdrop on a lotus leaf.
Pure and untouched as you move through life.'

'Before you leave, I wish to tell you something. Share this knowledge only with those who have sincerity, once they have cleansed their mind and body through the practices I have taught you,' Vini said.

'If you are confused about how to lead your life, you need to withdraw from the hustle and bustle of life, and spend some time alone and in silence. There are four contemplations you can deliberate upon.

'*Find your moral compass*. Whenever you are going through doubt, at the crossroads in your life, or in a dilemma, ask yourself where you draw the line between right and wrong.

'*Find your abilities*. What can help you earn a living and yet feel fulfilled? It is important to explore the abilities and skills you already have, which can help you come to a decision.

'*Find your passion*. You need to find what motivates you to wake up each day. You must seek a vocation that makes you feel good about yourself.

'*Find your joy*. When you love what you do, you become good at it, and if you can make a living out of it, you will be happy. But, primarily ask yourself where do you want to reach in life? Ambition is important, as it brings focus and direction to your life.'

'Can one lead a successful life simply with what one loves doing? Often, people are good at things they don't feel passionate about, and one cannot make sufficient money from things one loves doing,' Jay said.

'You will need to develop your skills in a focused manner, Jay. Find a few things that you are good at and choose something you really enjoy doing. Remember, what you love could be something you haven't done in years, and you may not be good at it any more. So, you will need to upgrade and update yourself. Similarly, what you were good at when you were younger may not be something you enjoy doing now, although it gives you an income.

'*Retrain your mind*. Be open to learning new things. If you try to force your way into something you would like to do but aren't good at, you would become frustrated and so will everyone around you. If you get into a job you are good at but do not enjoy, again you will be frustrated.'

'So what does one do, Vini? Nearly everyone seems to be stuck in a job that frustrates them, but since it brings much-needed income, one becomes trapped. Working a job one doesn't enjoy doesn't give anyone time to pursue a passion,' Jay lamented.

'There's a solution to this, Jay. It is possible to find joy and passion in things that one is good at but doesn't love.'

'Is that really possible, Vini?' Jay sounded surprised.

'When you seek pleasure out of any work that you do, you are bound to become frustrated, since the nature of our mind is that it gets bored of repetitive actions,' Vini stated.

'One can explore different ways to enjoy doing what one is already skilled at and what provides an income. It is far easier than to start learning something from scratch,' Jay concurred.

Vini laughed. 'That's a possibility. But it's unlikely to give you long-term satisfaction. You'll soon run out of ideas. But, when you do things with complete detachment, you do not seek pleasure as the reward for your acts. The reward is in the action itself.'

Jay was listening intently. Vini had revealed a great secret to him.

'It is a tough path, but it is possible. In the Bhagavad Gita it has been called the path of action, or Karma Yoga,' Vini said. 'But, it needs a mind that has been disciplined through yoga and meditation. In fact, this is the training you have acquired with me, Jay. You need to impart it to others now.'

'I guess I can always find something that I love doing and am skilled at, which will benefit people around me. But, will any of these things make me any money?' Jay wondered.

'In today's world, with a bit of skill and determination, one can make money in so many ways. You have a lot of skills, Jay, and I am sure you will be able to contribute greatly to society. Remember, Jay, you can earn what you need without too much effort, but you will become frustrated when you begin stoking your greed. Scale down your lifestyle, and you will have enough for yourself. When you earn more than your essential needs, help the needy, but not the greedy,' Vini said.

Jay was reminded of Raghav, whose family was totally content with the little they had. Raghav had no greed and lived a simple life. Jay could finally understand why his friend was happy. 'How do I know where to draw the line? Where does need end and greed begin?' Jay asked.

'We do not need much to be happy, Jay. There's nothing wrong with creating wealth. It's how you use it. The problems begin when one starts hoarding. If you have confidence in your abilities, you can create wealth again and again, and keep giving it away.

'Finally, if you want to find joy in your work, find like-minded people who appreciate you. Move away from places where you and your abilities aren't appreciated. Expand the practices you have learnt here, with me. Spend some time every day in self-development and serving those in need.

'There is great joy in creating wealth if you are doing it with the very purpose of contributing to humanity,' Vini concluded.

Jay remained silent for a while. He knew that it was time to leave.

'Will you go away, Vini? Will we ever meet again?' Tears welled up in Jay's eyes.

'I am not going anywhere, my dearest early-morning-airport-lounge friend.' Vini smiled compassionately.

'Can I come and meet you when I need your guidance?'

'I am always with you. I am in all that I have taught you. I am in your faith. You and I are connected forever.' Vini tousled Jay's hair, smiling.

'*Moko kahaan dhoondhe re bande,*
mai to tere paas mein.
Khoji hoye turat mil jaoon,
ik pal kee taalaas mein.
Kahat Kabir suno bhai saadho,
mai to hoon vishvaas mein.'

'Where do you search for me, dear seeker?
I am right next to you.
Seek sincerely and you will find me
within a moment of searching.
Thus says Kabir, listen, O wise brethren,
I live in your faith.'

Epilogue

The Way of the Millennial Yogi

Starting from scratch wasn't easy. Jay took up a job in a small firm. No one knew him there, as he had changed physically and begun to call himself J.S. Prasad. He kept to himself. But his work spoke for itself. The projects he planned went through like a charm. Within two months, the CEO wanted to meet him. He was given greater responsibility. Soon, Jay was told to attend client meetings. It would be just a matter of time before someone recognized him. People had heard of his past issues at ALSOL. Jay knew that he would have to deal with his past, someday.

Jay didn't react. Just like the interaction with his friends at the club, he asked for feedback and accepted advice. It was over six months before things began limping back to normal in his professional life. Word spread that Jay had resurfaced with a new company, and slowly, clients began connecting with him once again. But this time, Jay held on to his principles. He earned a fraction of what he was making at ALSOL, but he was at peace.

Shyam and Girish wanted to join him once again, but Jay refused politely. Pam reached out to congratulate him on his new venture, and they decided to meet for lunch. He was a bit surprised to see Arjun join them. Pam said that she and Arjun had come to an understanding. He had realized his folly. He wouldn't meddle in Pam's work any more. Arjun wanted to apologize and offered his help in setting up Jay's new venture. Jay refused.

* * *

Ritika turned up at his door one day, looking like a complete wreck. Sahil had dumped her, and she had asked Puja to take her in, but Puja had refused to even meet her. She and Timmy had blocked her number. Jay had no inclination to help her out, but this too was a remnant of the past that had to be dealt with. Jay gave her some money to buy food and the contact number of a hostel where she could stay rent-free. Ritika wasn't keen on this and abused him as she stormed off, crying. Jay didn't react. He realized that he really felt sad for her. She was such an unhappy soul. He hoped that she would find peace someday. It was then that he knew that it was finally over with Ritika.

Jay met Dharini, a dance teacher, while on his morning run and found her to be great company. She was a refreshing change from all the girls he had known in the past. She was deep into J. Krishnamurti's philosophy and lived a spartan life. Dharini had a like-minded group of friends who had no interest in an expensive and shallow lifestyle. They were into cycling, nature walks and trekking. Jay soon became a part of Dharini's group and rediscovered his love for bicycling. Jay felt comfortable spending time with her.

* * *

Jay created a unique method of training people to reclaim their lives based on Vini's teachings and his own life experiences. He rapidly became a sought-after self-help guru.

Vini and Jay met occasionally at the commune. Jay had decided to spend some time there every year. It was what he began calling his 'soul recharge'. Satish and Shubhra also enjoyed coming to the commune with him. Sometimes, Vini and Jay drove off into the mountains. They hardly spoke during those drives, but their silences were filled with contentment.

* * *

One evening, as Jay walked to the parking lot from one of his workshops, he heard a woman speaking in an agitated voice. '. . . that's impossible! How can you cancel the booking at the last minute? I'll complain to your manager. I have big clients coming! You don't get it, do you? This dinner is important! Damn!'

Jay saw the woman, who was dressed in a corporate suit and appeared to be in her late twenties, banging her fist on the bonnet of a BMW. She cried out as her phone slipped and clattered to the ground, right at his feet.

Jay bent down and picked it up. She looked flustered as he handed it to her. 'Looks fine. Nothing broken.'

'Thanks.' She smiled.

'*Often, when we let things be, they let us be.* I am Jay, by the way. Nice to meet you.'

'Oh, hi. Aditi Khanna. You look so familiar. Are you the famous Jay Prasad, by any chance?'

'In flesh and blood!' Jay nodded.

* * *

Somewhere, in a faraway land, at a seminar of mystic music, Vini was singing softly,

> '*Duniyaa jise kehete hain, jaaduu kaa khilonaa hai.*
> *Mil jaaye to mittii hai, kho jaaye to sonaa hai.*
> *Gham ho ki khushii, dono kuchh der ke saathii hain.*
> *Phir rastaa hii rastaa hai, hansnaa hai na ronaa hai.*'

> 'The world, as they call it, 'tis a magical toy.
> It's dust when grasped, it's gold when lost.
> Be it grief or joy, both are momentary friends.
> Soon, one enjoys travelling without laughter or tears.'

Acknowledgements

It has been a fascinating adventure writing my first book for Penguin Random House India.

Although I have been writing in various formats and languages for different media, I had no idea how books were published and all that went into making a book into, well, *the* book.

Firstly, Milee Ashwarya. I cannot thank you enough for making this book a reality. You watched over *The Millennial Yogi* as it grew from an idea into a complete manuscript. It has been an enlightening journey for me to have worked with you.

You have the gift, and see what others don't,
With words, crafting new worlds, as is your wont!

Nicholas Rixon, your astute editing suggestions have made the book shine. Working with you has been a unique experience. I love your candour and brevity.

Ourselves, into our tales, we always write,
Our happy songs bring laughter and delight!

Saksham Garg, dear friend, you have done so much for this book with your gentle suggestions and long conversations. Never let your goodness be compromised.

Often, we meet new friends by happenstance,
Strange are the songs and beats of cosmic dance!

Vineet Gill, your focused and calm demeanour, and your deep exploration of the nuances of Indian classical music have greatly helped nurture the story of Vini and Jay. I am certain that your contemplations of the mysteries of the khayal will bring joy to all your listeners.

A connoisseur of music, words and art,
Your gentle nature makes you stand apart.

There are many, many others at Penguin Random House India, led by Gaurav Shrinagesh, who have worked on unseen aspects of the book behind the scenes. I thank you all.

The myriad books you've made with skilfulness,
Have filled this world with joy and happiness!